ANGELS

Inspirational stories of

ANGELS

JT Stevens

Foreword by Gloria Hunniford

arrow books

Published by Arrow Books 2010

2 4 6 8 10 9 7 5 3 1

Text copyright © JT Stevens, 2010
Based on the programme *Angels* © Sky TV

JT Stevens has asserted his right under the Copyright, Designs
and Patents Act, 1988, to be identified as the author of this work.

First published in Great Britain in 2010 by
Arrow Books
Random House, 20 Vauxhall Bridge Road,
London SW1V 2SA

www.rbooks.co.uk

Addresses for companies within The Random House Group Limited can be found at:
www.randomhouse.co.uk/offices.htm

The Random House Group Limited Reg. No. 954009

A CIP catalogue record for this book
is available from the British Library

ISBN 978 0 0995 5646 6

The Random House Group Limited supports The Forest Stewardship
Council (FSC), the leading international forest certification organisation.
All our titles that are printed on Greenpeace approved FSC certified paper carry
the FSC logo. Our paper procurement policy can be found at
www.rbooks.co.uk/environment

Mixed Sources
Product group from well-managed
forests and other controlled sources
www.fsc.org Cert no. TT-COC-2139
© 1996 Forest Stewardship Council
FSC

Typeset in Sabon by Palimpsest Book Production Limited,
Falkirk, Stirlingshire
Printed and bound in Great Britain by
CPI Bookmarque, Croydon CR0 4TD

CONTENTS

FOREWORD

A parking angel is a somewhat unusual way of being introduced to the subject of angels, but my daughter Caron, whom I tragically lost to breast cancer in 2004, firmly believed that there were all kinds of angels for all kinds of reasons and we only had to ask for their help. After all, 'angel' means messenger and this is what they do.

Sceptical though I was, one day when Caron and I were out shopping, we were really put to the test in finding a parking meter, so with a wry smile I said, 'Right, where is your parking angel now?' You've guessed it, within seconds we were putting the money in the meter and duly parked in an otherwise overcrowded area that was crawling with traffic.

Trust me – at times I still call on that parking angel!

On a more serious note, Caron firmly believed that when you find an isolated white feather in an unusual or obscure place, it's an angel's calling card. Now, when I find one, I say to myself that's Caron's calling card.

Whether you're a staunch believer in angels or not,

fact or fantasy, there is an abundance of comfort in the theory and I now have jars of white feathers which I've picked up over the last six years since Caron's passing. I particularly find these white feathers when I'm with Caron's boys, Charlie and Gabriel. It's almost as if she is dropping in to say, 'Thanks, Mum, hope you're having a great time with the boys.' In a way, it's like she's a guardian angel to all the family.

I'm sure the majority of us have grown up with our grandparents or parents talking about the impact and presence of our guardian angel – and how many times have you heard someone say at a point of an accident or great distress, 'Thank God my guardian angel was looking after me.'?

As a child in Portadown in Northern Ireland, I went to church or Sunday school five times on a Sunday – mostly because there was nothing else to do in our town on the Sabbath, so that's where our social life lay. I was therefore surrounded by the environment of the church and religious belief and was very familiar with stories of our guardian angel, but it was only as an adult working in the BBC in Belfast, that I was to learn more about mine.

I was working on a radio outside broadcast one Halloween in the early 1970s and a sound engineer called me after the show to say how much he'd enjoyed the various interviews about the spirits of Halloween. He also alarmed me by saying, 'By the way, I'm a clairvoyant, I have the gift of second sight and, did you know you have a spirit who follows you around all the time – I particularly see it when you are in the TV studio. She sits at your shoulder and protects you.'

Well, at the time it freaked me out and I dismissed him as a bit of a weirdo.

Spin forward a few months to Christmas. I was in the studio on Boxing Day and he turned out to be my engineer, so there was no escaping him.

After the programme, we picked up on our previous conversation and, of course, I challenged him to tell me more about this spirit that accompanied me all the time. To my surprise and shock, he described my paternal grandmother in perfect detail – even to that little crooked smile she had, due to a stroke she suffered a few years earlier. Suddenly all my unease and cynicism disappeared. I felt very warmed to think of it and I still find it most comforting that she is my guardian angel watching over me.

Regardless of religious belief, and even if people totally reject the idea of angels, the majority are likely to subscribe to having a guardian angel and feel the consolation and hope it seems to bring. It helps them to realise that no matter how alone they may feel, there is a guardian angel at their side.

Of course angels have been with us for many, many centuries, they are rooted in all civilisations and they appear in all religions. Sculptors, poets and painters continue to have a place for angels and Christian prayers, even modern, revised and up-to-date prayers, still speak of them.

Even if people don't accept the possibility in principle that they might be part of our universe, nevertheless many will accept the theory that there is 'something else' – 'a force' leading to circumstances and influences which we just can't otherwise explain.

I particularly recall Richard, the soldier who appeared on the *Angels* programme, who, when he was in the army and serving in Northern Ireland, was caught in the crossfire of an IRA machine gun attack. He and his comrades managed to get out of the Land Rover they were travelling in safely, and his Lt. Colonel, who was now under cover, was already returning gunfire, when Richard, who had been trained for this kind of skirmish, but had never found himself in the reality and chaos of a real gun battle, started to go back into the Land Rover to get his gun from the gun rack. Suddenly he heard a voice say firmly, 'STOP'. Had he not listened to that voice, but continued to reach into the vehicle he would have been killed by a bullet which at that split second went right through the Land Rover and subsequently would have gone through his skull.

Richard accepts that his life was saved by that 'something else' that 'unexplainable force' and yet when I asked him if, after his experience he now believed in angels, he emphatically said, 'No'. You can read Richard's story in detail from page 91.

Foreword

During the making of the two series of *Angels* for Sky TV, I was fascinated by the popularity of the subject amongst the public and by the number of people with no religious or faith connections who were absolutely adamant that their lives and being had been touched and changed by their experience of an angel's presence.

Let's face it, images of angels are everywhere in modern day life – on greeting cards, ornaments, clothing, paintings and drawings, books, playing cards and there are even shops that sell nothing but angels. And in Gateshead in the north of England, we have the enormous imposing 'Angel of the North'.

Even in the absence of any religious connection, they're accepted. I particularly recall being at a social event for our family-run charity, The Caron Keating Foundation, and due to Caron's utter belief in angels, we had scattered the tables with white feathers, the symbolism of the angel's calling card. At the end of the evening in the middle of our farewells, I saw three really macho guys with the feathers sticking up out of the breast pocket of their formal dress suits. One said to me, 'I'm always going to keep these feathers in my pocket.' When I asked him how he would explain that to his mates on future occasions, he said 'I'll just tell them Caron sent them.'

Gloria Hunniford
September, 2010

For on the first day he created the heavens, which
   are above, and the earth, and the waters
   and all the spirits which minister before him:
The angels of the presence
The angels of sanctification
The angels of the spirit of fire
The angels of the spirit of the winds
The angels of the spirit of the clouds and darkness
   and snow and hail and frost
The angels of the resoundings and thunder and
   lightning
The angels of the spirits of cold and heat and
   winter and springtime and harvest and summer
And all of the spirits of his creatures which are
   in heaven and on earth.

Book of Jubilees 2:2

GLENNYCE ECKERSLEY

Glennyce Eckersley is an internationally acclaimed writer and broadcaster. With a background in science, she worked for many years in the medical research laboratories of ICI. She took a career break to live and work in Los Angeles for several years before returning to England.

Her first book, *An Angel at My Shoulder*, was published in 1996 by Rider Books, and she has written several more since. Here Glennyce explains how she came to believe in angels, recounts some of the amazing stories she's heard, and how she believes that angels take on many different forms, from the spirit of loved ones who have died, to the traditional image of a bright shining angel with wings. Angelic encounters, she says, differ from person to person, it is up to each individual to take notice and have faith.

Glennyce Eckersley hasn't always believed in angels. Although now her belief is unshakeable, she used to be a hard-nosed scientist who wouldn't believe anything without incontrovertible proof. The turning point, you might think, must have been some kind of amazing angelic experience. Perhaps she saw an angel, or even heard its voice? No, her belief in angels actually developed very slowly. It didn't become the cornerstone of her life until she looked back and saw a thread of angelic experience running right the way through it.

'When I first started to write I was very unconvinced. I don't see angels and I've never had the dramatic experiences that some people have had but, looking back, my life has been filled with these incredible coincidences.'

Glennyce was born in Manchester and she was always interested in travel and discovery. When she was young she spent several years in the United States, working as a nanny and then travelling around the country. She has also worked as a technician in ICI's medical research laboratories. Eventually, though, she got a job at a theological college in

Manchester. It was devoted to the teachings of the eighteenth-century theologian and scientist Emmanuel Swedenborg. He was a firm believer in angels but even then Glennyce was not convinced. It wasn't until much later that she began to delve further into the spiritual world.

'Although I worked at a theological college, I didn't have a theological outlook on anything. I came from a scientific, research background. You can't make up stories when you're doing research. Everything has to be checked and double checked.'

However, even when she was doing cancer research, Glennyce was starting to wonder whether there was more to the world than biology and physics.

'We used to put clinical trials on, and I met some wonderful people, many of whom were terminally ill, and I wondered why, in the face of such adversity, they had a strong faith. Also, as we discovered more and more, I couldn't help wondering whether there was a grand plan or design for the world. But although I asked the questions, I didn't really pursue any answers.'

It wasn't until she started hearing stories about angels that she became more interested, and that, again, happened purely by chance.

'The college used to have a stand at the Festival

of Mind, Body and Spirit in London. We used to try and think of a theme for the stall, to make it look attractive and one year we decided to use angels as the theme because I'd noticed that there were a lot of books coming from our sister college in the States about angels and angelic experiences. This was in 1996 and interest had just started to pick up – there'd been a few things on television and in the papers and there had been a spate of films about angels. I decided that it couldn't just be happening in America, so I started asking around and got my friends and colleagues to ask around as well. From that initial investigation, I got four stories, which I wrote up and put into a leaflet together with a little bit of information about the theology of angels, and we left them on the stand for people to pick up.'

Glennyce thought the stories were very interesting and she was convinced that the people she'd interviewed were telling the truth. However, she still wasn't sure whether what they were describing were real angelic experiences, or whether there was a logical explanation.

By coincidence the Festival of Mind, Body and Spirit was held just up the road from the offices of publishers Random House.

'One of the people who picked up the leaflet was

Judith, an editor from Random House. Judith had had an hour free and had decided to pop into the festival to see if there was anything interesting. Not long after the festival Judith called me and asked me to come and see her. She told me she had liked my leaflet and would love to publish a home-grown book about angels.'

Glennyce was intrigued but she wondered how easy it would be to find enough stories to fill a whole book. She was also a little embarrassed, and wondered what people would think of her writing about something so odd. At that time, although there was a great deal of interest in angels in the United States, the idea hadn't arrived in the UK in a big way. Glennyce was further daunted by the tough deadline.

'When Judith mentioned when she'd like the book, I slithered off my chair!' The deadline gave Glennyce only five months to find the stories and write the book.

Nevertheless she started asking people at the college and elsewhere if anyone had ever had any unusual or supernatural experiences that might have been caused by angels. To her surprise the stories just flooded in. They also came from the most surprising sources.

'If anything convinced me that it was meant to

be it was when I was staying with a friend in London. She was a professor at London University, very hard-nosed, very matter-of-fact, and she happened to be giving a dinner party that evening. I was desperately hoping that no one would ask what I was doing down in London, but of course sooner or later somebody did. I was sure that they were all going to laugh or tear me to shreds in some way when I admitted that I was writing a book about angels and angelic experiences, but instead my friend asked if I'd ever heard the story of the time her mother saw four angels, and after that the stories kept coming. By the end of that evening I had eight stories from six people, the sort of people you would never dream would believe in angels, and from then on word spread. Back in Manchester I gave a couple of talks about angels at the college and I got so many stories from there. And it just kept spreading.'

But the event that really convinced Glennyce about the existence of some other power or spirits was when she spent an evening with a friend and had an experience that was impossible to explain. It was not long after she'd been asked to write her first book.

'A friend and I were both working with young people at the time and we used to have regular get-togethers to swap ideas and talk about what we could do in terms of artwork and music and keeping them all interested. I didn't realise my friend was a very spiritual person and had, for a long time, believed in angels but never discussed it. We were sitting in her house one night and it was cold and the room was quite dim, with just the fire and a couple of lamps lighting it. It was very cosy, and she was telling me about one little girl in her group who was very, very needy and very disruptive and she didn't realise, until she gave her a lift one night, how run down the area she came from was nor how deprived the child was. She was clearly deprived of everything, including love. So instead of trying to control her and tell her off, my friend started giving her affection and a bit of responsibility. Mainly, though, she'd just give her a hug. And she said that the girl had blossomed like a little flower after that. This got us talking about the meaning of love in people's lives and how those who've had no love of any description do grow up slightly damaged. We all need love. And, as we said this, suddenly the room, just for a few seconds, was filled with light, and even more astonishingly, we both felt a strange tingling sensation. It felt like when you hear a lovely piece of music and you get shivers down your spine. Something very strange had happened, and my friend said she was sure it was an angel.

'I told the principal of the college, who was a theologian, about it and he explained that angelic experiences come in all shapes and forms. People don't often see angels but there's a whole raft, a myriad of experiences, that are angelic. He thought my experience, as I was clearly not in distress and wasn't in need of an angel in the normal sense, was that I was being given a message: I had a job to do. The strange thing is that he didn't know then that Judith had asked me to write a book, but I was shocked, and that was the first time I really believed that I was being asked to do something.'

From then on Glennyce started seeing more and more signs and symbols of angels in her life. Looking back it was as though she'd been heading in this direction ever since she was born.

'A few years ago I was giving a talk in Wales and somebody asked me if I was Welsh, because my name is Welsh. I explained that although I'm not, my grandfather was from Anglesey and he chose my name. She said she wasn't at all surprised because Anglesey means "Isle of Angels". My other grandfather had property in Manchester, and during my pre-school days he'd take me and my siblings along to his office in Angel Meadow in Manchester. And if I look back there's a pattern of angels and angel places and angel topics running through my life that I'd never noticed before. When I got to my late teens I got itchy feet and I wanted to travel and I went to live in Los Angeles, the city of angels. Everything, places and people, were all connected with angels. Which I didn't notice, of course, until I started writing.'

Gradually, little by little, Glennyce was starting to believe. More than anything else, it was the many stories that she heard that convinced Glennyce that there are angels looking over us.

'The dinner party experience, when those highly intellectual people told me their wonderful stories instead of laughing at me, convinced me. And over fifteen years I've met and interviewed hundreds and hundreds of people. Plus I've received emails, and almost all of them are from nice, normal people. And in many cases they've never told their story to anybody before. So I started by believing the people and then I saw the signs in my own life.'

Having become convinced that Guardian Angels are real, Glennyce then became evangelical about spreading the word. She wanted to tell everybody that they too could invite the angels into their life. It was just a question of faith. There was one question that needed to be answered, though: what are angels?

Surprisingly, Glennyce is not a big fan of the word 'angel', or at least not in the way in which it's often understood.

'The term angel can put people off because the word is associated with a saccharine image of fluffy things on greetings cards, on top of Christmas trees or little artefacts with angels on. They trivialise the whole thing. Angels are not always fluffy; I know of one lady who saw an angel with armour on, which is a very biblical image of an angel.'

For Glennyce there's much more to angelic experiences than the traditional image of a winged saviour, even though she knows that that is how some people experience angels.

'It's the tip of the angelic iceberg, people who see angels. Although it must be incredible, it's very rare. Most of the people I've met who have actually seen an angel have often been in real dire straits. For example, a man in the first book I wrote was just about to jump off a cliff when an angel appeared in front of him. Another man was nearly drowned in a swimming pool and an angel came underwater, lifted him up and placed him on the side. He was a big bloke and it would have taken more than one

11

person to lift him out. Nobody could have picked him up and lifted him on to the side. So that was an angel. But it seems as if it's the extraordinary situations where angels appear like that, I don't think they just appear willy-nilly.'

Although Glennyce finds these stories fascinating, they're not the main focus of her work. She is more concerned with helping people to appreciate subtle signs of angelic influence, which she says are much more common.

'I think we receive what we can cope with and what we need. So if we just need a gentle reminder that somebody's there then it's quite likely we'll see a sign from nature, a rainbow at a time when you're down, or hear some music or see a bright light. But angelic experiences seem to be bespoke – tailor-made to our circumstances.'

Perhaps because of this there is a lot of debate about what exactly angels are. This is particularly true within the church.

'There's a religious debate raging at the moment. The traditional churches, such as the Roman Catholic Church and the Church of England, would probably say that angels are a race apart; they've been created by God in heaven and when somebody needs them God makes sure that they come. The other side of the debate says that they are people who've gone on to heaven and they're there to help us. Many of the examples in this book include those who have experience of loved ones still helping them. I think that maybe both are right. I wonder if there could be a sort of hierarchy, including angels who've never lived on earth, but I believe that there are also many, many angels looking out for us who are people close to us. That's probably why most people say they're not at all frightened when they see an angel. They have this lovely feeling of warmth and love as opposed to when they see ghosts and they're scared and there's a cold atmosphere.'

So the theory that Guardian Angels are relatives who've died and gone to heaven but are still able to come back to this world is definitely one that Glennyce subscribes to.

'Certainly that's what people have told me and it does make sense from lots of different things that I've read. I started to read about the subject quite extensively at the theological college and I think the overriding opinion is that angels are people who've lived. The majority of people I've interviewed who've seen angels have recognised them. It's been their mother or their partner or somebody that they know really well. That would fit in with the belief that the Guardian Angel is somebody close to us looking after us.'

For Glennyce, angels are something universal. She's noticed that, as her books have been translated into different languages, she hears different stories from different countries.

'People in the United States tend to be much less inhibited than we are. They're very keen to tell you their story. There are a lot of very dramatic stories and they're only too happy for everybody to hear them. The English are a good deal more reticent. In the Catholic countries the experiences are tied in with religion, it's often the Virgin Mary who has sent the angels. And also, Catholics have often had experiences in church, which is pretty rare for this country. I've also found that different nationalities will see different angels. For example, I spoke to a Brazilian lady who was living in London and she was very homesick. One night she was very distressed and missing home terribly and she said the room was filled with angels dressed in bright colours and dancing to Brazilian music. So she saw what was comfortable for her.'

Glennyce has discovered that belief in angels is shared by all kinds of different religions and cultures. It's not just a Christian phenomenon. In other parts of the world they have different names for the same thing.

'Certainly indigenous peoples, like the Native

Americans and the Aborigines, have completely different names for them; spirit guides and things like that. But if you look into it they're obviously angels, it's just a label, really. There are angels in Buddhism and Islam. Lots of them even have the same names; Gabriel comes into many different religions.'

As well as angels being sent to earth as guardians, another theory is that angels are within us.

'Swedenborg talked about everyone having an inner angel. He believed that we are here to be angels. This is a training ground. And when we die we go on to be angels. Within us we've got an inner angel that we have to exercise and be the best person that we can while we're here because we're training to be an angel in heaven. But it is all about love. The more you love people the nicer you can be, then the more people are kind and nice to you. You're helping the love go round and flow.'

Although these theories are interesting to talk about and to read about, for Glennyce they miss the point. Her view of angels is very much simpler. Although she's been very successful thanks to the increased interest in angels since the turn of the century, she is slightly dubious about some aspects of it. She thinks that some books and courses on offer have gone too far.

'I try and keep it real. I try and keep my feet on the ground. I think a lot of people take it far too seriously. Last week I gave a talk at one of the local libraries in Salford [in Manchester] and seventy people turned up. They were asking me questions like, "How do I summon angels?", "Is there a ritual?", "Why haven't I seen an angel?" I told them that they were probably trying too hard. There's no magic formula. A lot of people want to know about the hierarchy of angels and which angel is responsible for this and which is responsible for that. I don't see that as relevant in everyday life. People are looking for comfort. They're looking for reassurance. I think it's really quite simple. If you trust, suspend disbelief and open up to the idea, then things do happen. I think there are a lot of signs, quite significant signs, in nature and music. There's nothing necessarily extraordinary about the things that happen but it's all in the timing.

'People don't need to go to any great lengths, or read every book about angels under the sun. Nor do they need any rituals for summoning an angel. They're smart enough to find you, I think.'

As somebody with a scientific background Glennyce is still very interested in the idea that science might explain the phenomenon of angels one day. She wonders whether angels might exist in other dimensions. Is it possible that they are simply beings that can move from one dimension to another? It sounds like something out of science fiction but she says that it's a theory with some heavyweight support.

'In an interview, one of the physicists at Manchester University who works on the CERN experiment in Switzerland (the large hadron collider) said that they're hoping the CERN experiment will provide the answers to all sorts of questions. His research is into gravity. Scientists can't understand why gravity is so weak, it should be much more powerful than it is. So he believes that gravity is dispersed among other dimensions. He's convinced that there are many, many dimensions in the universe – he feels he has identified seventeen. He has suggested that we could discover all kinds of things in these other dimensions.

'Swedenborg talked about the afterlife as being like another dimension,' Glennyce says. 'He said it's just a case of slipping over into this other world. But once we were there it would be very familiar. There would be houses and people. It is literally another dimension. So I sometimes wonder whether angels are in one of these dimensions. Because if you look at the light spectrum, there's so much light that we can't see. The visual spectrum is very small.

For example, we can't see something like ultra-violet or infra-red light but we can certainly feel its presence and its effect. Maybe that's true of angels. Maybe at certain points they can alter their light-waves and their vibrations because they are pure energy and light. At that point we can see them. Perhaps science and other things are all coming together and we're getting nearer the answer. There are many scientists who think that science and spirituality can go hand in hand.'

More important than what angels are, though, is how we can connect with them. That's been the basis of Glennyce's work ever since she wrote her first book. She believes that, far from being some kind of exotic and extraordinary phenomenon that can only be seen at our darkest hour, they are all around us. We can see signs of them in our everyday lives.

One of the phrases that Glennyce has often used is 'angelic synchronicity'. It means coincidences that are more than just coincidence. She thinks that, very often, things that appear to be normal can have special significance depending on when they appear.

'It's all in the timing. There are many times when I look back at an event and think, if I hadn't gone there at that time, I wouldn't have met such-and-such a person. Sometimes there's such a clear pattern and I think that's how my angelic experiences are.'

The classic example that she often gives is the sight of a white feather. We have all seen white feathers around but, according to Glennyce, if you see them at an unusual time or place they can be significant. She regards them as an angelic calling card.

'If at one of my talks I ask whether anyone's seen a white feather in unusual circumstances, then usually there will be at least twenty people out of seventy who will have seen a feather when they wouldn't expect to. Often you see them when you need confirmation that everything's going to be all right.'

Glennyce believes that white feathers are the most common form of communication from angels. She thinks that, in their hearts, people know whether it's just a feather or something more significant.

Feathers are not the only sign, however, and Glennyce remembers one angelic sign that was particularly poignant.

'Many people have experiences with music. Two or three years ago now I was doing a talk and a woman wanted to talk about her twenty-year-old son who'd committed suicide while he was at university. Two years down the line she hadn't come to terms with his death and she was desperate for confirmation that he was okay, that he hadn't just disappeared into nothing. She needed a sign to help her come to terms with his death. She had come to my talk because she thought maybe I could give her an answer, maybe the angels would answer. I told her that I couldn't give her a definitive answer, but that she needed to try to open up to the idea that if you believe in the angels and you trust them there will be a sign.

When the woman left, Glennyce watched her from the window as she walked into the car park.

'I saw her getting into her car and then all of a sudden she got out and came rushing back, tears streaming down her face, she could hardly speak for crying. She explained that she had got into her car, and asked the angels for a sign. Then, when she switched on the car radio her son's favourite song, a little-known song by the Manic Street Preachers, came on the radio. It was one they'd played at his funeral, but because it was an album track it was never played on the radio.

For Glennyce, this kind of 'coincidence' is the most common sign of angelic influence. Just hearing a song that reminds you of somebody doesn't mean anything on its own; it's the circumstances in which you hear it that are significant and, just as importantly, your own attitude. If you make the decision to believe in 'synchronicity' then you will probably experience it much more often.

For the lady in Glennyce's story that would not be the last time that she heard the Manic Street Preachers' song.

'The lady's sister lived in Australia and had asked her to come and visit, but she hated to leave her son's grave, which was in the churchyard at the end of her road. But after hearing the song on the radio, she realised it was a sign from the angels that he was all right, so she decided to go to Australia. While she was at the travel agent a couple of days later, the same music came on. Many people would say that that was just a coincidence, and maybe it was, but for her it was a mind-blowing coincidence.'

The main focus of Glennyce's books is in teaching people to notice the difference between simple coincidence and 'angelic synchronicity'. Although some people believe that there's no such thing as coincidence and that everything is pre-ordained she believes that some coincidences are much more significant than others. For example, if you're thinking about somebody you've not seen for ages and then you bump into them that can be pure coincidence. But there are other, more spiritual signs

21

that can be enormously significant, such as for the woman mentioned above, and Glennyce believes that people need to open themselves up to the possibilities and take notice of what they see around them. For Glennyce, spiritual coincidences are very obvious.

'There's a big difference. I think small coincidences can point us in the right direction because it's been brought to your notice. You can think, "Well, maybe if I looked into this a bit further then it would be significant." For example, people see butterflies a lot when someone's died and they've thought that's a message from someone who's gone. And you might think, "Well, that's just a coincidence, because it's a summer's day and there are loads of butterflies." But, if you trust it a bit, the bigger signs, the spiritual signs, can happen. I definitely believe in the idea of synchronicity. It's a case of taking notice.'

One of the questions many people ask about angels is, why would they save just one person when there's so much death and tragedy in the world? One answer Glennyce gives is that some people are saved for a specific reason. They have a task to accomplish before they die. For example in this book, Rita Lyons firmly believes that to be the case with her. Glennyce has heard many examples of this as well.

'I know of a lady whose daughter was involved in a serious car accident, but she walked away without a scratch. The next morning this girl's car had a white feather on it and they both had a really strong feeling that she'd been saved for something special. She's now a qualified doctor working in the third world, and she is convinced that this is why her life was saved that day.

Glennyce accepts that this argument isn't a comfort for others whose loved ones die while they are still young. 'It's hard to understand why some people are saved and some people aren't but it's one of life's enigmas I'm afraid.'

But one reason why Glennyce's books are so popular is that many people think it's possible to invite angels into your life, to make it more likely that they will help you.

She also believes that there's a reason why angels have become more popular in the last ten years. She thinks that our rapidly changing, noisy, crowded world has made people more fearful and more interested in spirituality.

'At the turn of every century there's been a resurgence of interest. So the millennium was a big deal. People wanted reassurance for the future, but I also think, during the last century more than any other, there's been a blizzard of technology and material goods. People have so much now, but ultimately material goods don't make you happy, and I feel there has been a bit of a backlash against the modern materialistic mentality. Science has been incredible, there have been terrific strides in our search for knowledge, and the twentieth century was wondrous, things have advanced like never before. But even after all that, after the dust has settled, people are still searching for something. If they're not happy inside themselves then no amount of money or houses or fast cars is going to change that. That's not to say that people who have these things are unhappy, but I doubt the possessions are the main reason for their happiness.

'People like to know that there's something there for them, something comforting. They don't have to join a religious organisation. Church attendances have dive-bombed so conventional religion is not addressing people's issues. But people still have that spiritual vacuum, they're still looking for something. And an angel is one to one – you don't have to sign up, you don't have to go to meetings, you don't have to give money, they're there for you at all times. I think there are many different ways to tap into the same energy and we're just putting different labels on it.'

That's why Glennyce's books have been so

successful. She tries to help people discover their own angel. But she's always keen to emphasise that people have to find their own way. She's a little dubious about some teachers and organisations that claim they can help with 'spiritual development'.

'Many of them are too intense. They are very expensive, too. And it can be a struggle for people to find that kind of money. You can find your own way, by reading, obviously, but also by believing, living in the moment, and not trying too hard. Simply ask for help and it is there. It's quite easy, really. People complicate things too much.'

Her advice for getting in touch with your angel is much simpler and doesn't cost any money at all.

'Meditate. It's absolutely perfect. If we look at all the things that became popular towards the millennium, such as Reiki, reflexology and yoga, they all have a spiritual element to them and most of these disciplines incorporate meditation. I have several friends who've lost someone close to them and they've gone to the Quakers. The Quakers believe in sitting still and being quiet, which is a form of meditation. Meditation is one of the ways to bring things to you. My suggestion is that people should light a candle, and have five minutes of peace on their own. If they find it hard to meditate, then concentrate on the flame and allow the thoughts to come. That's probably the easiest way to receive messages. You can't expect to light a candle one day and receive messages the next but it builds; it just requires practice, and you need to be clear in your mind. Spiritually, meditation can take you quite a long way. I like to meditate once a week if I can.'

Sometimes people misunderstand what her writings are about. They see belief in angels as a kind of religion in itself and that's something that Glennyce discourages. Nor is she keen on the modern idea that you can order angels to deliver you prosperity, as though they were bringing a take-away.

'I don't like the idea of people praying to angels. This is something that the church is very against because they are only messengers. You pray to God and if you need an angel he'll send one. There's nothing wrong with asking angels to help you in a situation. But asking for a better house or the lottery numbers doesn't work!'

The best example of the benefits of believing in angels comes from Glennyce's own life. Not only did she become a successful author, she's also been a regular on TV. That, too, she says was an example of 'angelic synchronicity' at its best.

* * *

Glennyce's TV career really took off when she was invited to go on ITV's *This Morning*.

'After I'd written my first book, *This Morning* got to know about it. Fern Britton was very keen on angels, so I was asked to do an interview. Everyone was worried that I'd be petrified, but when it came to it, I didn't feel scared at all. A little nervous, but I felt as if I was where I was meant to be. I saw it as another medium for getting the message across. It was the loveliest experience and I've done an awful lot of television since then.'

Following that, she was asked to be the expert on *Angels*.

'It was funny because when there was a meeting between the production company and Sky, I discovered that out of the four people in the room, three of them knew me and had worked with me, although they didn't know they were all connected to me in this way until they started discussing who to have as the angel expert. It was a big coincidence. I never in a million years thought I'd end up on TV, especially not as an angel expert. It's always been very comfortable and I've enjoyed it but if somebody had said twelve months before the first book came out that that's what I'd be doing I would never have believed them. I thought that, even when I was writing it, six months later it'd all be over and done with. I never thought that anything would come from it. It's been astonishing.'

It's also meant that she's heard some amazing stories, not just the ones that appeared on the show.

'The most interesting thing that happened to me was at a press day when a journalist from a magazine went to see Nicky Alan, the medium. Nicky Alan told her that she was getting messages from her father, who had died just two weeks before. She gave the journalist a very personal message with instructions about the direction she should take, which was just amazing. After she'd spoken to Nicky, the girl came to see me and she was feeling very tearful and emotional. She told me she was shocked by the messages she received and she now wondered whether her father was an angel. As she said this, the room filled with the most incredible fragrance, which floated around us and then went away quite quickly. We were in a stark room in the middle of a big building with no windows and no flowers or anything. At first she thought perhaps I had some candles burning, but I explained that I thought she was having her own angelic experience. It was very moving and dramatic.'

There were other stories that were equally dramatic, perhaps too dramatic to be shown on screen.

'One of the most stunning stories I've heard involved a lovely young couple. It had always been the man's dream to learn to fly a helicopter and have one of his own. They were a very successful couple, and he did manage to buy himself a helicopter, but his wife wasn't happy about this. She couldn't help worrying. But he learned to fly regardless and when he finally qualified as a helicopter pilot, he decided to fly up to Liverpool to show his instructors.

'His wife was a great believer in angels and she gave him a little angel figurine to take with him. She watched from the window as he took off, but something went badly wrong: the rotors stopped turning and the helicopter plunged to earth and burst into flames. She rushed outside fearing that he would have been killed, but there was her husband, standing on the other side of the helicopter looking at it in utter bewilderment. A dog walker who witnessed the accident said that as the helicopter fell, the door flew open and the pilot literally flew into the air and landed on his feet. It's an incredible story, and the man can't remember anything about it, but his wife is convinced an angel saved him, and I have to agree.'

At the moment Glennyce is working on another book. It will be her tenth, including those that she's co-written with American author Gary Quinn. Her books have been translated into numerous languages and through them she's given a great deal of support and comfort to many people. Along the way she's also found it easier to make sense of her own life. Before she became involved with angels she says that she had a sense of missing something.

'I always felt I wanted to do more with my life. Something that might benefit more people; the sense that I hadn't contributed as much as I was able nagged at me. So to be able to tell people's stories is an incredible privilege, and it is heart-warming to think that others have found comfort from them, even if they've never had experiences themselves.'

RUBEN CARRIL

There are some events that change your life beyond recognition. Ruben Carril's life changed one sunny morning on the Santa Monica Highway, and in many ways it changed for the worse. However, Ruben will tell you the opposite, that his life became immeasurably better that terrible day because it brought him into contact with his angel, and forced him to reconsider his life. Here is his incredible story.

It was a gorgeous sunny morning, and Ruben Carril was doing what he liked best: riding his motorbike. He was on his way to Santa Monica, and with the Pacific Ocean calling him, the early morning sunshine just starting to warm his back, and a gentle breeze blowing against his face, he felt at peace at last.

He hadn't been at peace when he wheeled his bike out of the garage that morning. He'd had yet another argument with his wife the night before and he'd woken up in a bad mood, but the ride on the motorbike was reviving his spirits, as it always did. The last few months hadn't been easy. He was thirty-eight and he'd been married for four years, but already his marriage seemed to be falling apart. Even the business that he'd built up, which had always been a source of pride and hope, had run into unexpected problems. He knew he was in a rut, and he needed a fresh start. However, the decision to ride to his meeting, at least, seemed to be the right one, even if he hadn't taken it entirely for the right reasons.

'My wife said: "Why don't you take the car

33

today?" And partly because I was angry and partly because the motorbike always relaxes me, it seemed like the right thing to do. And anyway, my doctor had told me that I needed to learn to relax more to bring my blood pressure down. I'd tried therapy and various other things, but my motorbike was the only thing that really helped me wind down. But I knew it upset my wife so that just added to the tension between us!'

The sky was already a bright blue and, although it was still cool, Ruben could tell that it was going to be a beautiful day. He stopped thinking about the argument and started thinking about the day's work. Ruben's company provided pigeon control services, putting up spikes around buildings. He'd built it up from nothing and, although there were problems, he loved being his own boss and getting to travel around southern California.

'I completely forgot about the argument, I was just thinking about the day and enjoying the ride and looking forward to work. I was going to Santa Monica and I had another appointment further up the coast and it was a wonderful opportunity to get out on the bike.'

His serene mood wasn't broken until he got further into central Los Angeles where there were more cars and lorries on the road and he found himself surrounded on all sides on the four-lane freeway. He started to feel a little tense as he pulled up at some traffic lights.

'A car pulled up next to me and was trying to squeeze by me and I thought, "What the heck are you doing?" So I revved my engine. You know how loud a Harley can be? Even if the guy was deaf he would've at least felt the vibration.'

But the driver in the car, now dangerously close to him, didn't look round. He was just staring straight ahead as though he couldn't see Ruben's enormous Harley.

'His side mirror was a few inches away from my handlebars. Today, I wonder what I would have done differently if I could do it over again. I think I would probably just smash his windscreen. But instead, I just kept revving, hoping he would notice me. He had his head in his hand. He didn't even turn to look at me. He was two feet behind me and I had to look over my shoulder at him but he didn't even look at me.'

When the lights changed Ruben hoped that he'd be able to pull away and put a bit more distance between him and the driver. Instead the car edged forwards. It seemed that he still hadn't seen him.

'When the light turned green he tried to go round me and his mirror hit my handlebars. I vividly remember the back of his mirror, which was plastic, cracking and breaking.'

The Harley Davidson is a very stable motorbike but it was moving very slowly and there was nowhere for it to go. It could only topple over and there were cars on one side and an enormous lorry on the other.

'I started to wobble and I couldn't speed up because there were cars all around me, so I tried to get control but I just couldn't recover my balance, and I went underneath the lorry that was next to me.'

It was every motorcyclist's nightmare but even then Ruben thought that he might be able to escape with relatively minor injuries. The traffic wasn't moving fast and if he was hit by a car he knew he would probably survive.

'It was a long lorry and I was pretty far back,' he says, 'and I thought I could jump off my bike because I'd rather get run over by a car than a lorry. Instead I got half my body out from underneath. My motorcycle went down and I was next to it and the lorry driver didn't know I was back there so he carried on going.'

The lorry kept on rolling remorselessly down the freeway. However, when the wheels hit Ruben's motorbike they didn't roll over it, they just pushed it along the road, pushing him with it. Sparks were flying upwards as the chassis scraped along the concrete but, although he couldn't get away, by some miracle, he hadn't been crushed under the wheels.

'The back wheel didn't run over me,' says Ruben. 'It just pushed my motorcycle along because it didn't have the traction to go over it. And I was next to it. My back was being dragged along the concrete. It was tearing my clothes, ripping into my skin, there were horns honking and people yelling.'

Luckily Ruben was well protected. He often went out on his bike wearing only light clothing because it was so warm in California, but on that day he'd put on his full protective gear. If he'd just been wearing a T-shirt things could have been even worse.

'I always wore boots and I always wore jeans and a helmet but it was cool enough that I wore a leather jacket and thank God because that really helped to save my life,' he admits.

Meanwhile, the drivers who'd seen Ruben fall were desperately trying to get the lorry driver to stop. They couldn't know that he was in an impossible position. He couldn't escape, he was dragged thirty yards along the road and yet when the truck did slow down it was the worst thing that could possibly happen.

'Finally a car pulled out in front of the lorry to get him to stop,' says Ruben. 'And as the lorry slowed down the tyre finally got traction and went over the motorcycle and over the lower half of my body.' As the lorry went over the motorbike the sparks ignited the petrol tank, which immediately exploded.

Ruben had never been scared of dying. He had great confidence in his own skill as a motorcyclist and in his ability to avoid trouble. As a kid he'd dreamed of being a stuntman so he wasn't scared of taking risks and, after leaving school, he'd spent two years in the US Air Force and then another four years in the National Guard. Even so, nothing had prepared him for the pain that he was experiencing. The drivers going past could only look on in horror. Most of them just continued on, too shaken, scared or confused to stop. Only one person got out of his van, abandoning it on the outside lane to rush over to try and help him. He carefully removed Ruben's helmet and goggles and then they could only wait until the emergency services arrived.

'I remember lying there with somebody holding my hand saying, "Is there anything I can do for you?"' says Ruben. It was a man called Doug, who was later to tell him that he'd had similar experiences before, once pulling somebody out of a burning car, while other passers-by looked the other way.

'I said "Call my wife. And I think that's one of the things that helped me stay conscious – that he interacted with me. He was asking me questions that I had to think about. I tried to give him my wife's number, then I realised I'd given him mine. So I tried again, but I was in excruciating pain. I remember lying there thinking: "Oh God, please make the pain stop, please help me, oh God, God." And then I heard sirens coming and I vaguely remember people working on me and two fire engines and an ambulance and police. It was crazy.'

Thanks to Doug, Ruben didn't lose consciousness and that might have saved his life but he was in horrible pain and when the paramedics started working on him it didn't look like there was much hope. He'd suffered terrible injuries to his legs and his pelvis as well as being badly burned. The shock alone should have been enough to kill him. However, it was almost as though, even then, there was somebody looking over him who didn't think it was time for him to die.

The paramedics managed to free him and, as they lifted Ruben on to the stretcher and up into the ambulance, he was still conscious. They were all

around him, desperately trying to save his life
when suddenly he saw something, or someone, that
would change the way he saw the world for ever.

'I remember them putting me into the ambulance,
I looked up and that was when I saw the angel.
He was looking down at me very calmly while
everybody was working frantically. He was very
peaceful, very calm. He put his hand on me and
said: "Everything will be OK, I'll take care of you,
I'll watch over you."'

The angel was like nothing Ruben had ever seen
before. It was above him in the ambulance and yet
the paramedics didn't seem aware of its presence
at all.

'If you had to describe the perfect-looking man,
this was what he was. He had a square jaw, and
long wavy hair down to his shoulders, but he was
very rugged looking. He was muscular, not like a
body-builder, much more natural than that, and he
had massive wings, you could see the muscles in
the wing. It was an amazing experience.'

In a different context, to see something like that
might have been terrifying, or at least startling, but
Ruben felt an intense tranquillity take him over
when he heard the angel speak. From that moment
on he was convinced that somehow, despite the
odds, he would make it.

'I never felt like I was going to die but until then I didn't know that I was going to live. When I saw him I knew that everything was going to be OK. I was absolutely 100 per cent sure that everything would be fine.'

After seeing the angel it was almost as though he'd been given permission to rest. He didn't feel that this was the end, and he knew that if he closed his eyes, it would only be a matter of time before he woke again.

The ambulance, sirens screaming, rushed the unconscious Ruben through the traffic to the hospital. It was touch and go as to whether he would survive. With such severe injuries the first few hours, the first few minutes, even, were crucial. The surgeons' first priority was to stop the loss of blood. He was taken into the operating theatre but, at that stage, all they could do was try and keep him alive. When Ruben's wife and family came to the hospital the doctors told them that there was very little hope. He needed to have a second operation as soon as possible but he was very weak and it was clear that he was going to lose his leg.

'When they were wheeling me to the theatre for my second operation they told my wife to take a good look at me because it might be the last time she saw me alive. Everybody at the hospital prepared my family for the worst.' Ruben was given a 5 per cent chance of survival.

As they'd feared they had to amputate his leg from the hip. It was an operation of extreme complexity and it was not his only injury. As his family gathered by his bedside afterwards they thanked God that he'd made it this far but they were warned that he was still a very long way from safety. Ruben's parents are devout Christians and they knew that, literally, all they could do was to pray. They also rallied not just their own church congregation, but also the congregations of friends, and asked them to pray for him. Ruben remembers how moved he felt when he found out later about the dozens or perhaps even hundreds of people who had prayed for his safe recovery.

He remained in a coma for six weeks. On the day his eyes at last flickered open his parents were by his bedside. He was still horribly close to death and yet for the first time they had more than just a glimmer of hope. The doctors, however, warned them not to get their hopes up too much. He was still at death's door. He also had to face the brutal reality of having lost his leg. He'd always been the strong, active type and inevitably they were worried about how he would cope with the news and the shock. To their surprise, though, he didn't react as they'd expected. He seemed strangely calm.

'When I found out that I'd had to have an amputation, I was upset for a few minutes but I was suddenly comforted with the calming thought that this decision was the right one,' he says.

They had to remove the leg. It was the only way he could have possibly survived. He accepted that and was just happy to still be alive. Even then, though, there was still a long way to go.

'When I came out of the coma they had to put me on dialysis, and I had two nurses looking after me round the clock. My chances of survival were absolutely minimal but the funny thing is I never felt like I was going to die.'

The first people he told about what he'd seen in the ambulance were his parents. As Christians they accepted the Bible's account of angels coming to earth in times gone by but at the same time the story he told them was astonishing. They were incredibly moved and yet, having seen his recovery against such impossible odds, they didn't doubt him for a second.

'My parents are very religious people and they were just blown away by it,' Ruben recalls. 'I was always a believer but I used to go to church once a month. All my life I've had a strong belief in Jesus

Christ but I never really believed in angels coming to earth, although I know that the Bible says that there are angels. I knew that angels existed but being able to see an angel and hear him was a miracle in itself.'

The next few months were hard in ways that Ruben could never have expected. It wasn't just the physical pain that he was still suffering, or the trauma of having to learn to walk again without his left leg, his whole world had been turned upside down. The accident could have brought him closer to his wife but instead they drifted further apart. The marriage, which had seemed to be crumbling even as he wheeled his bike out of the garage that day, was now barely functioning. It was an incredibly hard time and yet the vision that he'd seen in the ambulance, the certainty he felt that there was more to this earth than just the physical world, proved an enormous source of comfort and strength.

'I really felt protected,' he says. 'I know now that we do have a Guardian Angel and he does protect us. That gave me a confidence that I wouldn't have had otherwise. While I was recuperating after the accident and learning to walk again that confidence helped me a lot because that was when my marriage was failing. I was pretty much left alone. There were times when I gave in to despair, but then I'd start thinking about what had happened and the people who had prayed for me, and it gave me the strength to carry on.'

Whenever he felt depressed he could also look at the cards and letters that he'd received. When he awoke from his coma it was to a room full of warm wishes. Knowing that people cared made an enormous difference.

'The number of get-well cards I received was incredible, they probably make a pile that is six or seven inches tall. To this day I still think about all those people who prayed for me. I really do think that prayers work and are answered.'

Slowly Ruben regained his strength. With the help of a small army of occupational therapists, nurses, doctors and other medical staff he learned to walk again. He overcame his physical problems, but the real enemy now was boredom and loneliness. He was used to being able to do anything he wanted. If he felt down he could just wheel out the Harley Davidson and take off across California. Now, with his wife estranged from him and his daughter from a previous relationship moving across the country to live at her mother's house, he was increasingly isolated. His friends and his family did everything they could to help but, even with people around him, he still felt very alone.

He'd always been a romantic, the kind of person who has the idea in their head of the 'perfect' woman but he'd lost faith that that person existed. He hadn't, however, given up on finding some kind of companionship. One day he decided to post his profile on an Internet dating site. He had no real expectation of success. He felt that some women might reject him because of the loss of his limb and, having recently come out of an unsuccessful relationship, he wasn't sure he could easily trust anybody again.

Thousands of miles away, though, in the UK a German woman called Sabine Mai was also browsing Internet dating sites. She'd been through her own painful divorce and, like him, she was wondering whether there was such a thing as true love. Her career was going well, she had her own successful company but she was just as lonely as Ruben.

'She found my profile and we started emailing each other,' he says. 'I wasn't looking so much for a long-term relationship, I was just looking for companionship.'

By coincidence Sabine worked as an occupational therapist. Ruben was inevitably impressed by this, having experienced occupational therapy first hand and knowing its value, but the connection helped them in another way, too. She was used to meeting people who'd lost limbs or who were paraplegic. She understood that it didn't make any difference to somebody's personality and she wasn't intimidated by his physical problems.

Over the next week or so they exchanged innumerable emails and eventually spoke on the phone. It all seemed to be happening incredibly fast and, at one point, Ruben wondered whether it was all too good to be true. After everything he'd been through it seemed impossible that he could find somebody this easily. Surely his luck couldn't have changed that much? 'We started talking about life and things that we had in common and after only two and a half weeks, I started thinking that everything was too perfect.'

In the back of his mind the thought lingered that she might not be who she said she was. On the Internet it's easy to pretend to be something that you're not. They had exchanged photos but still Ruben worried that Sabine might not be the person she claimed to be.

He phoned her and all the emotion that had been building up since they first contacted each other came flooding out. Ruben couldn't help crying and told her that he couldn't believe she was who she said she was. Sabine just said that if he couldn't believe her over the Internet, then she would just have to come and see him in person. So when she put the phone down she booked a ticket to Los Angeles, justifying it to herself by saying that she'd never been to America before. If she got there and it didn't work out, well, at least it was a holiday and an adventure. What did she have to lose? For both of them, though, there was an enormous feeling of expectation. They'd half fallen in love just through their emails, through understanding how much they had in common with each other. How would they feel if they met each other and that spark wasn't there? Was it possible that the connection that they felt on the phone could be there in person?

Even though it was Sabine who was flying halfway across the world Ruben was taking a risk, too. He'd built up his hopes so much, and after the struggle he'd had to put his life back together, one more let down would have been a bitter blow. Since the day of his accident, though, his attitude to life had changed. Not only did he appreciate how fragile life could be, he also had a sense of being protected. The certainty that he had a Guardian Angel watching over him made him feel much more confident about taking risks and about opening himself up to new experiences.

There was something else, too. While he was in the coma he'd had another vision. It didn't have the same impact as seeing the angel in the ambulance but it did give him a message that he has never forgotten.

'I had a lot of hallucinations in my coma, and I remember one where it was completely black and there was a building as big as an aircraft hangar and I walked towards it. Inside there was a water-fall of light, a continuous shower of light, with the silhouette of a person inside. The shower of light wasn't very big, maybe a metre and a half wide and you could put your hand in it and it would continue to fall. So I passed through this wall of light and there was a person dressed in a robe with long hair like a biker. I crouched down so I could see the face, but it kept changing, man, woman, white, black, it didn't matter, the face was constantly changing. It looked at me and said: "My child you look but you do not see, you search but you do not find, close your eyes and open your heart." When I came out of my coma I remembered that immediately and I wrote it down.'

The message to 'open his heart' was a very moving one for Ruben. He'd been through an incredibly harrowing experience, both physically and mentally. He'd got through that only to find that the person he once expected to spend the rest of his life with was no longer there for him. It would have been natural to have retreated into himself, to try to avoid being hurt again. Instead he decided to open himself up to another psychological wound at a time when it had been a struggle just to rediscover a purpose for his life.

When Sabine arrived at the airport in LA neither of them knew what to expect. There was a danger that the image that they'd created of each other wouldn't match the reality. How could it? All they had to go on was a picture, some emails and a few phone conversations. They didn't have a 'real' relationship at all. Inevitably, both of them had doubts. But when Ruben met Sabine they vanished almost instantly.

'The first time we met she gave me a hug that absolutely melted my heart,' he recalls with a smile. 'She came to my house and we had dinner and it was as if I'd known her all my life. When I was younger I had this idea of how the perfect woman would be, how she would treat me and how she would care about me and she fitted all those ideals.'

The fact that Sabine had taken the risk of coming out to see him made it even more special for Ruben.

He found it extraordinary that somebody would do that. Her daring and decisiveness matched his, and the bond that they'd developed in emails and on the telephone was even stronger in person.

'She flew out – only to be with me,' says Ruben. 'It was absolute love and at that moment, the first time I saw her, I knew that I was going to spend the rest of my life with her.'

They spent a wonderful few days together in Los Angeles and then, as soon as she was gone, they started planning when they would see each other again. A couple of weeks later Ruben flew to England to see her and this time they spent ten days together. It wasn't as long as they would have liked but it was enough. At the end of the ten days Ruben had made up his mind. She was the woman that he'd always dreamed about and he couldn't live without her.

Sabine felt the same way. The only dilemma they had was that they lived thousands of miles apart. Her life and the business she'd worked so hard to build up was based in England. More importantly, so was her daughter. Meanwhile Ruben's parents and his own daughter lived in the United States. It was clear that one of them would have to make a very difficult decision. For Ruben the decision was made harder by the fact that his mother was unwell and his relationship with his daughter, who now lived across the country, wasn't always easy. She'd moved away from Ruben when she was fourteen after she'd started hanging around with the wrong people and her grades had started slipping. Since moving to live with her mother, she'd been doing much better at school. Although Ruben was happy that his daughter was doing well at school, he didn't see her as often as he wanted to any more. Also, because his relationship with her mother wasn't perfect the tension affected her, too. In the end he decided that he had to follow his heart and go to England. The battle he'd been through to recover after his accident had taken its toll on his daughter as well and it was better for both of them if he started again.

Just a few weeks after they'd met, Ruben headed to the UK to be with Sabine. Initially it was quite a culture shock. 'We don't have villages in LA,' he laughs. 'We just have the city!' But his relationship with Sabine went from strength to strength. He was able to bring his business expertise to her occupational therapy company and, to his delight, over the next few months his relationship with his daughter greatly improved, too. When she graduated from high school he flew out with Sabine to be there with her. They'd planned to spend as much time as possible with her, see the sights and then go home. When they got there, though, another thought popped into his head.

'We had decided that we weren't going to get married; we agreed that we didn't need to. We knew that we were going to be together for ever so what was the point of getting married?'

But, while they were in the States they couldn't resist the romance of the occasion. One morning they got on a plane and flew to Las Vegas. 'We left in the morning and came back in the afternoon, literally,' he says. 'We got married, hopped on a plane and flew back and nobody missed us.'

They didn't even tell their daughters what they'd done. It was an impulsive gesture that was purely about affirming the love that they felt for each other. Nobody else was involved at all. It was as though everything that had happened since Ruben saw the angel in the ambulance had been leading up to this moment. He couldn't believe how his luck had changed.

In a fairytale this would have been the happy ending. Ruben had gone through the worst imaginable experience and yet seeing his Guardian Angel seemed to have changed everything. It was truly as though he'd been protected and blessed from that moment on.

However, he had a strong feeling that he couldn't carry on as if nothing had happened. If he'd been saved, he thought, it must have been for a reason. Living with the certainty that he had a Guardian Angel protecting him he couldn't just go back to his old life, however rewarding he might have found the work he did before. He needed to make a difference and to justify the fact that he'd been chosen, against the odds, to live.

The first part of his new life was simply about doing the things that he'd always wanted. He was determined to help Sabine build up her company but he also began working on numerous projects of his own.

'My career is the company that Sabine and I have, that's number one,' he says. 'She's the brains behind it. She's the occupational therapist and without her the company can't run but she trusts me to do the taxes and the marketing. Number two is to finish the book that I'm writing about my experiences, and to find a publisher and get it published.'

As well as this, though, Ruben has also found work in television and film. He appeared as an extra in an advert, did voiceover work and appeared in a short film. Even more importantly, though, he wanted to rebuild his relationship with his daughter.

'That's changed so much since I moved to the

UK because I'm in a better place,' he says. 'When I left I left a lot of good behind but I left a lot of bad behind as well, and I think my daughter realised that I wasn't in a good position even before my accident. The accident just amplified my situation.'

After he flew out with Sabine for his daughter's graduation it was a new start for all of them. Having confirmed their love for each other in Las Vegas, Ruben and Sabine still felt that there was something missing. They hadn't told their respective daughters about their marriage and they wanted to make them feel like part of the new family as well. With that in mind Ruben asked Sabine to marry him all over again. And in July 2010, Ruben, Sabine and their two daughters took a trip to Greece, where Ruben and Sabine got married all over again in front of the two people who mean most to them in the world.

The one thing that could have made Ruben stay in the USA was the love he had for his daughter. It was only the fact that she was seventeen when he met Sabine that made him feel that moving to another country wouldn't be so difficult for them both.

'I'm here for my daughter because she needs me. She tells people all the time, "Don't ride a motorcycle because I almost lost my dad." When I hear her say "I almost lost my dad" it makes it so worthwhile knowing that I survived. I don't care what condition I'm in. I'm alive and I'm here for her.'

But beyond his own personal happiness, and that of his family, there was something else that Ruben felt he had to do to make the best of his unexpected chance at life. He wanted to try and prevent the kind of horrific accident that he'd had from happening to anybody else.

When he had his crash the moment that caused him the most damage, that almost killed him, was when he went under the wheels of the lorry. Had the same accident happened in Europe, rather than in the United States, it's possible that he wouldn't have been dragged under at all.

'In Europe all large trucks have sidebars to prevent cars, bikes and motorcycles from going underneath them,' he says. 'In the United States they don't.'

When he realised that, he wondered whether it would be possible to do something to save lives and prevent other people going through what he went through. The obvious answer was to persuade the US government to change the law.

'I've got my own website called motorcyclesafety.org and I'm trying to lobby congress to pass a law to make it mandatory for all lorries to have sidebars. I have photographs of me under the lorry and I made a video on YouTube for drivers to be more aware of motorcycles and for motorcyclists to be aware of the traffic around them.'

Although he knew that he could never persuade people to take fewer risks on their own behalf, he did want to make them realise the wider repercussions. It was only after his accident that he understood how much his own decisions affected the people that he loved.

'When they get on a motorbike, every motorcyclist knows the risks that they're taking. What they don't think about – and this is what I was thinking about when I was lying there asking God to help me – is their family. Motorcyclists don't take into consideration the fact that if they get injured it doesn't just affect them, it affects everyone around them who cares about them. If somebody's paraplegic or quadriplegic who's going to help them? You're making decisions for people who don't have a say. If I get on a motorcycle now, I know that I have to take Sabine's feelings into consideration because if something happens to me she's going to take care of me. Is she willing to do that? Am I being selfish making this decision for her?'

Ruben was inspired by the response that he got from his campaign. It wasn't just touching other motorcyclists but all kinds of people who were struggling in their lives, after accidents or through ill-health.

The video has had over 100,000 views and many people have left messages about how the video has affected them. One man said he sold his motorbike the day after watching the video, and another, an AIDS sufferer, found the message on the video inspired him to live his life more positively. Others have told him that his video has saved lives. Ruben is just happy it's had some effect. 'I think that if I had to go through all this to save one person's life, just one, then it was all worthwhile and I would do it all over again.'

For all his bravery, when Ruben came out of the coma and realised that he needed to learn to walk without his left leg, he went through some tough times. He felt that, despite their kindness, none of the people around him really knew what he was going through. Because of this he actively searched out other people who'd suffered limb loss to get some kind of support and understanding. That was why, when he moved to the UK, he volunteered his services to the Limbless Association.

'I'm trying to give something back. The Limbless

Association, which is based in Roehampton in London, supports people with limb loss and their families. I'm a volunteer so when there's somebody who's had a similar accident or similar limb loss they'll ask me to give this person a call so I can give them moral support. I wish I'd had that after my accident, but I had to find it on my own. The Limbless Association is a place where people can go for answers and for hope. They work solely on donation so I'm trying to raise at least two thousand pounds from sponsorship and people sponsoring me for my skydive in July.'

There was more to his skydive than just raising money, however important that was. It was a sign that he hadn't given up. He was still able to live, not just a normal life but an extraordinary one.

'I did the skydive to show people that, if you lose a limb, life doesn't have to end. I'm going to continue to live my life the way I did before. I still walk. I just walk differently. I still do things, I just do them differently.'

The feeling that he had a Guardian Angel looking over him totally changed the way Ruben saw the world. It made him 'seize the day' in a way that he'd never managed before. From skydiving to taking the decision to move to England he felt like he was capable of so much more than he had been.

'It has completely boosted my confidence to know that I'm being taken care of. I know that things happen to you. I don't think that I'm going to live for a hundred years because I've got a Guardian Angel. I can still subject myself to things that are going to damage my body and I don't think that he's going to protect me from things like that. I think he protected me because he was told to, because my life isn't over. There are still things that aren't finished, according to God.'

Ruben's religious faith is also something that was changed by his experience. He'd always identified himself as a Christian but he'd had doubts and uncertainty. Now he felt like he had something solid to believe in. It was an experience that he felt evangelical about but, at the same time, he doesn't want to force his beliefs on people who don't share them.

'I do try and share my story as much as possible. I will often answer people who leave comments on my YouTube with: "God bless you and your family." I don't know these people's religious backgrounds and I'm apprehensive because I don't want to offend people but, since my accident, I say things like "God bless you" more often. I don't go to church more since it's happened but I reflect on my beliefs more now. It definitely strengthened my faith, without a doubt. I'm one of those people that knows, 100 per cent, without a doubt, that when I die I'm going to heaven. There's no question about it.'

There were two ways Ruben could have reacted after his accident. He could have felt bitter and angry. He had every right to feel that way. The car driver should have seen him. The lorry should have had protective bars stopping motorbikes sliding underneath it. But instead he chose to react the other way. He was just grateful for being alive and being given a second chance. He doesn't know whether that is because of what he saw in the ambulance but he surprised even himself with how little bitterness there was in his heart. He couldn't even bring himself to hate the driver who'd knocked him under the wheels of a lorry and then sped off without stopping to call for help. Whoever it was has never been caught, and there was no evidence to help police.

Some people might have spent the months after the accident trying to find who did this to them but Ruben had more important things to think about. 'He's the one who has to sleep at night. I have no remorse. If I ever saw the guy I wouldn't have anything bad to say to him. I'd have questions for him. I'd ask: "Why did you hit me when you knew I was there? Why didn't you stop? I don't understand. Explain it to me." But I'm not angry, no. I find it really weird that I'm not angry but I never have been. Even when I came out of my coma I wasn't angry. The only time I was angry was before he hit me because I wanted him to know that I was there.'

Perhaps because he's found an inner peace Ruben has also been lucky in another way. After terrible accidents many people suffer from post-traumatic stress disorder. It's a condition that can manifest itself in many different ways, from sleeplessness to nightmares and worse. He says, though, that he didn't experience anything like that after he came out of the coma.

'Weirdly enough, so many people suffer from post-traumatic stress disorder but I've never ever had that. I just feel so fortunate. I do on occasion have a slight flashback, an image that pops in my head, like I'm back in that scene, but it's only for a second and it doesn't bother me. I know it's just a memory.'

It must have helped him to know that not everybody was like the driver who knocked him down and fled the scene. Although the celestial angel that appeared to him in the ambulance might have been the most memorable, the more prosaic, human angels were just as significant. Ruben can never forget the gesture of Doug, who just happened to be passing by.

'He was going to work and he didn't see the accident happen. He was four lanes away and he saw my motorcycle blow up and this big blue ball of flame go up in the air. He heard me screaming and he got out of his van. He didn't even put it into park, the guy in the passenger seat had to, and he ran across. He was just somebody who happened to go by. He was at the right place at the right time.'

Those kind of everyday miracles are what Ruben wants to help achieve with his charity work and his campaigning. He feels like he's been given a second chance and he doesn't want to waste it. In a funny way he's thankful for the accident now.

'I wanted so badly to wipe the slate clean, even before the accident. I just wanted everything to go away so I could start over and I didn't feel like I had the strength and the ability to do that. The accident was my rebirth, it was the beginning of my new life. I look at my accident almost as a blessing. I'm glad it happened. Only good things have happened to me since then.'

But of course the accident itself couldn't be described as a good thing. He went through terrible pain and then a gruelling struggle to rebuild his life. It was the vision that he saw that day in the ambulance that changed everything, a vision he wouldn't have received had he not gone under the lorry that day. There are some people, though, who while admiring Ruben's courage and perseverance, say that it was just a hallucination or a trick of his mind. Ruben is adamant that that is not the case.

'I feel bad that I was the only one that saw the angel. I wish somebody else could have seen him because I know he was there. It was crystal clear. How can you hallucinate something so calm and peaceful and tranquil? I could see him vividly. It wasn't like my eyes were closed and I imagined it.'

That feeling of tranquillity has stayed with him and allowed him to achieve incredible things since the accident. If Guardian Angels do exist then Ruben's story must be the strongest proof, not because of what he says he saw but because of what he did afterwards. 'People think that your life ends after an accident. But mine has just begun.'

JOAN BULLOCK

Some people may never see their Guardian Angel, but despite this they are aware of the spirits and angels of others. For Joan Bullock, the belief in the existence of spirits is an important part of her life, and with this comes a belief in angels. She may never have seen one for herself, but her grandson Billy certainly has, and there have been crucial times in her life when her prayers were answered. Was this the work of angels? Joan can never be sure, but one thing she is sure about is that there are special forces looking out for her family, and she shares her experiences with us here.

In the delivery room at Stepping Hill hospital in Stockport, Manchester the only person who wasn't worried was the expectant mother. The midwife had been joined by a junior doctor and they were peering anxiously at the heart monitor. It was beeping steadily but there was something wrong. Meanwhile, Joan Bullock, who'd been so proud of becoming a grandmother, was trying not to show her daughter that she was worried. Joan had some medical experience, having worked in a cancer research laboratory as a technician and then as a nutritionist and reflexologist, and she could see that there were problems.

'My daughter wanted me and her sister with her for the birth to assist her – she didn't want her husband to be there as she thinks it's not a man's job – and, to start with, everything was going quite normally, but after a bit the junior doctor came in the room and stayed and I wondered why he didn't leave. Then I looked at the monitors I could see that every time my daughter had a contraction the baby's heart was failing. As soon as the contractions subsided his heart picked up again.'

Joan was known in her family for being cool in a crisis, but as the tension rose she found it difficult to hide her concern. Meanwhile, Lynn still had no idea that anything might be wrong. This was her first pregnancy and she was impressed by how many people had come into the room to help her. Even when the baby was born, silent and white, she didn't realise that this wasn't normal.

The awful fear and anxiety of that moment is still clearly etched on Joan's memory. 'He wasn't breathing, he wasn't moving and there were obviously problems,' Joan recalls. 'They sent for the paediatrician immediately and took the baby to the resuscitation unit where they tried to get him to breathe and get his heart going again. I was quite calm on the outside but all I could think was: he can't be dead, he hasn't had a life yet and this can't happen to my daughter.'

Meanwhile Lynn was oblivious to what was unfolding. She was exhausted but happy that the staff were taking such good care of her child. She had no way of knowing that his life hung in the balance.

'She thought that all babies needed resuscitation,' says Joan. 'Her sister was in tears but she dashed off to make a cup of tea so that Lynn couldn't see how upset she was and neither I nor the staff said anything.'

The baby was silent for only a few minutes but it felt like a lifetime to Joan. She didn't believe that he could be dead but she knew that this wasn't normal. 'There was no noise, no movement. He wasn't blue; he was white. I don't know how far gone he was but they gave him adrenaline to get the heartbeat going.'

Nothing seemed to be working. Then, as the baby lay there, limp and silent, Joan saw something.

'Out of the corner of my eye I spotted a misty ball of light at ceiling height, and I had the horrible feeling that this was his spirit on the way out, so in my mind I begged the spirit to give life to the little body, because we would know how to look after it.'

And at that moment, the baby began to cry.

Joan hadn't always believed so strongly in the supernatural. As a child growing up in Lancashire she'd been interested in nature rather than religion. She'd gone to Sunday School, mainly because her friends went, but in her early years it wasn't a big part of her life.

Still, she wasn't surprised to see the light in the delivery room because, as she'd got older, she'd come to believe more and more strongly that at times of great energy and emotion, such as births or deaths, spirits can appear. When both her parents died in 1987, one after the other, she took great comfort from a feeling that they were still with her.

'My mother died first, and I was with her but I didn't see any spirit then. But three days after she died I was awake in the bedroom and I saw a sparkly green light, like you'd see coming off a sparkler. I didn't hear the voice, it was only in my head but it told me that my dad was going to die of a cerebral haemorrhage and that I wouldn't be with him when he died. I asked if he could at least be in hospital so he wouldn't be alone.'

Not long afterwards Joan's father fell over and had to go into hospital. It seemed like he would be fine but, sadly, he had a stroke. Joan, a trained reflexologist, performed reflexology on him and he recovered feeling in his arm but he wasn't getting much better. Eventually he developed pneumonia and, about a month after his stroke, Joan received a phone call from the hospital telling her that she needed to come in.

'It was about five o'clock in the evening and I was called into hospital because they thought that he was going to pass away,' she says. 'At about one o'clock the next afternoon I felt a hand on my shoulder, but there was nobody there and then I had an image that the hand of this spirit was touching my father and I realised that this was my mum who had come to be with us. I'd been sitting with my dad for so long and I was exhausted so the nurses suggested I take a break. They promised to make him more comfortable while I was gone. I'd only been outside for half an hour when I got a feeling that I must go back in.'

When she went back into the hospital it was too late. Her father was dead.

'I thought I could hear breathing but it wasn't, it was just his energy vibrating around him. Then I saw a bright white light and straight after a beautiful purple light. My hands started tingling and I lifted them above my head, feeling the energy rising up them. That's when I knew: Mum had come for him.'

To lose both parents in such a short space of time was a terrible blow for Joan. That night she felt almost crushed with sadness and she didn't know what to do with herself. She was exhausted and felt very alone. It was then that she had an even more extraordinary experience.

'That evening I was lying on the floor in front of the fire and I saw the faces of Mum and Dad above me. They said: "You can't come with us, we've come to close your aura." Those weren't words they'd use, it was something I might say, but that was what I heard them say in my head. I had a kitten at the time, and it rubbed itself all the way around my body. And that was the kitten closing my aura.'

Since then, Joan's parents have remained as a presence and a source of comfort. She also says that they're useful in a much more prosaic way.

'I do communicate with my father quite often. He used to be an electrician and I once, after he had died, I asked him to mend my fridge freezer because it was rattling. The next day, the rattling had stopped and it's never rattled since. Then there was a friend who couldn't get a DVD player to play. She'd tried everything, so I asked my dad to fix it, and although there was a big group of people in the room there was no one near the DVD player and it just started playing music. He gets quite useful at times! If there's a job I don't know how to do I ask Dad to guide me, and I get a message of how to do it.'

Joan finds herself talking to her mother at times, too, and even has a special relationship with her cat.

'My mum's good at finding things if I've lost them. That's the way I talk to her. The cat and I communicate very well, too. He either knows what time it is or he knows when I'm thinking about him. I don't have to shout at him. I just have to think about him and he'll come!'

Joan puts her unusual sensitivity to spirits down to her experience as a reflexologist and years studying tai-chi. She feels that these experiences made her more open to the paranormal.

'I've been a reflexologist for thirty years and I'm very sensitive to energy. I can feel if people have got a pain. I put my hand over it and it goes warm and the pain disappears for people. I've always been aware of energy. You might call it "spirit", I just call it energy. That's life force. I don't usually get visual images but at the point where people are dying or at the point of birth I do seem to see things.'

That day in the delivery room, though, Joan didn't just see the spirit, she tried to communicate with it. She says that it was almost as though she was trying to reassure it. Despite the desperate situation, she was strangely calm. As it hovered in the corner of the room there seemed to be more life in its cobweb of light than there was in the baby. Joan, though, was adamant that her daughter was not going to lose her first child like this. She was sure that he would survive.

'I don't know whether people are born with the

spirit in them or whether the spirit's hanging around. I've heard of people who've had operations or almost died and they say that they saw themselves from above. So to me it was like his spirit had left his body and it was observing what was being done. That was my observation; other people have suggested the light was his Guardian Angel. My appeal was to that spirit, to give that little body life.

As soon as the baby cried Joan looked away from the ball of light and when she looked back it had gone. At last Joan's calmness left her, she couldn't stop the tears as waves of relief and joy rushed over her. It felt like a miracle. She was so proud of her daughter and of her beautiful newborn grandson, Billy.

Billy was immediately a source of delight to both his mother and his grandmother. He was a happy, tranquil child. However, his traumatic birth was by no means the end of the story. When he was a few months old they started to realise that something was wrong.

'We brought him home and he was gorgeous, a very placid, happy baby. But after a while we saw he wasn't sitting up unaided. Then he wasn't moving when he was left on the floor. He wasn't making any attempt to crawl. So I used to move his hands to show him how to get going and get down on to his tummy but as time went by he still wasn't walking. He didn't walk until he was about three years old and even then he couldn't walk unaided.'

It was becoming increasingly clear that Billy would need special assistance. He struggled with his balance and he seemed awkward and uncoordinated. Eventually he was diagnosed with dyspraxia. People with dyspraxia often have difficulties with motor control, with things like walking, writing and even talking. The family had no way of knowing for certain whether his difficult birth had caused mild brain damage but it seemed possible.

Despite Billy's problems, neither Joan nor Lynn despaired. If he had problems it just meant that they would all have to work a little harder to solve them. And, gradually, by sheer determination, grit and special attention from his family and professionals, Billy was able to conquer many of his problems.

'We took him to a cranial osteopath, and after five treatments he started to walk unaided. I'd also been given useful advice about nutrition that might help children with the difficulties that Billy had, and with a lot of support, he made progress at school.

Sadly, however, although Billy wasn't necessarily

worse at school than other children, he was different and he was bullied and, when he was fifteen, they decided that a specialist school might be able to help him.

'The special school was much better for him. He's got the most compassionate nature. There were children there who had all sorts of problems. And he saw what their need was and helped them. He learned sign language so that he could communicate with the deaf. Those that could pronounce sounds but not words he taught to pronounce "Billy". He just seems to have a way with children that have got problems. They like him being around at special school because he sorts the others out and engages them in conversation. He brings them out. His ideal job would be caring for others.'

Billy never wanted to be the person who everybody else was fussing over. He never regarded himself as disabled because nobody in his family ever treated him that way. Even when he was unwell he felt much more comfortable being the person who was helping everybody else, rather than being helped himself.

By his teenage years Billy had conquered many of his problems and learned to cope with some of the others. However, he did experience night terrors that disturbed his sleep patterns, and he suffered from epilepsy, but he didn't let these problems stop him from living his life to the full. Every day he was learning more and becoming a young man. Joan still worried about him but she did what she could to help. As a Christian this often meant praying for him and asking her church to pray for him. As she's got older her faith has also got stronger. It's something that's been with her since she was a child but it's grown in importance in the last few years.

'For fifty years I hadn't been to church and then four years ago I started going with some friends to a church where the vicar was particularly spiritual. His teaching wasn't about dogma and creed it was more about love and fellowship. He inspired me. The first time I went I couldn't take communion, because I've not been confirmed, but I went up for a blessing, and when the vicar put his hands on my head I went really, really hot. And when I stood up I burst into tears. He's got a special energy about him. He reckons he can see angels.'

At the church that Joan attends these kind of beliefs are not rare. Even those members of the congregation who have never experienced angels or spirits are not surprised to hear that others have. People who have experienced loss are particularly receptive.

'When I talk to people at church they don't see it as anything unusual, especially if they've suffered a bereavement, they become more open to things. There's a lot of energy around death. That life force is not going to be destroyed. I don't think it stays around very long but it's definitely there.'

In her form of spirituality a belief in healing is very important and it's something that she's tried to harness for Billy.

'I went to a ceremony at an ancient Longburrow where they buried the dead and these burial sites are usually on leylines [lines believed to connect important monuments in New Age philosophy]. We did a healing ceremony, and we watched the sun setting and the full moon rising. We made a healing circle and they asked if anybody wanted to put a name into it, so I put Billy's name in, and when I got home I asked my daughter how Billy had been on that Friday night. At this time poor Billy was having night terrors and fits and Lynn was disturbed every night. I was desperate to help in any way I could. Even if they didn't know it. When Lynn told me that that night he'd slept for nine undisturbed hours, I was so grateful to whatever had helped them. Neither of them knew I was sending Billy healing, but it worked.'

It was a blessed relief to Billy and his mother,

but then when he was eighteen years old Billy became ill again and this time it didn't seem like any kind of healing, spiritual or medical, would be enough to help him. Once again it seemed like he'd need a miracle to survive.

After being sick for a while, and being sent home by the GP, Billy was finally admitted to hospital with double pneumonia and septicaemia. No one knows how the pneumonia could have caused the blood infection, but Billy's life hung in the balance.

That night, as Billy battled for his life, Lynn had a disturbing dream. She saw a vision of him in his hospital bed surrounded by white light. She was terrified that the lights were angels who had come for him.

It was a chilling vision for a family who'd come to regard angels as a normal part of birth and also of death. Lynn had heard the story of the spirit of her grandmother appearing at the deathbed of her grandfather and she desperately hoped that something similar wasn't happening again. However, the reverse was true.

The next day when Lynn went to see Billy he told her that he had three angels working on him. Billy had grown up with the concept of angels, because his mother would always comfort him in his night terrors, when he was terrified of falling, by telling him that angels would catch him. And maybe she was right about that. Because although Billy was exhausted by his illness, he was confident that the people around him were doing all they could to help him get better, and that what the staff couldn't do, the angels would help with. All he had to do was lie back and let them get on with it.

It was a very worrying time for the whole family but they were comforted by Billy's innocent confidence that everything would be okay.

'He's eighteen and he still believes in Father Christmas and he was determined to get home before Father Christmas came because he wanted his presents. And he actually came out of hospital on Christmas Eve so he was home for Christmas.'

It seemed there definitely was somebody watching over Billy. But the most astonishing revelation was when Billy told his family that he was relieved he wouldn't have any more fits. And sure enough, he's not had an epileptic fit since. When the consultant asked him what had stopped his fits, Billy just said, 'The angels.'

Billy's incredible sensitivity to other people may

well be the clue as to why he is so open to his angels. Joan also thinks that Billy has an uncanny gift for knowing what people are thinking.

'When he was about three he'd come into the room and then immediately go back out. He'd say "I'm going to get on your nerves in a minute!" He could sense that my daughter was in a bad mood or something. He's very good at picking up atmospheres.'

Joan, too, often feels that she knows what he's thinking.

'Sometimes Billy doesn't want you to speak to him. Sometimes I'll go into a room and ignore him because I know that that's what he wants.'

But there's more to the story than just Joan, Lynn and Billy. Joan believes that in her family there have been other strange occurrences that science cannot easily explain. It all goes back to the interest in spirituality that she started to develop as she got older. One of her most life-changing experiences was when she first discovered reflexology – the practice of manipulating the hands and feet to influence the whole body.

'I was a technician in a cancer research laboratory. After that I did a post-graduate diploma in dietetics and I became a dietician for a while. I did an Open University degree in Medical Laboratory Science.'

Nevertheless she was also interested in religion and spirituality and she was open to different ideas and ways of doing things. After she split up with her husband when she was thirty-five, she began studying things more deeply.

'I started going to a series of lectures that were being held near where I lived. They were on various medical topics, and one night the lecture was about reflexology. That night changed my life. I was very impressed with it, and I decided that I wanted to study and practise reflexology. And that's what I did.'

Working in cancer research Joan had experienced the miracle of modern medicine, but also its limitations. It was particularly heart-breaking when she had to see children who weren't going to make it.

'I had one special little patient who had leukaemia who used to call me the "thumb lady" as I would take blood samples from her thumb. Her mother used to tell me that she was always a bit better after she'd seen me, and I think that was because of the energy I would give off.'

Joan has seen how, sometimes, a gentle touch can be as important for patients as anything else. As a dietician she was interested in helping people to help themselves but she also realised that some people simply needed love and attention. And she feels strongly that her experience as a reflexologist is one of the things that has made her more sensitive to the spirit world. Her work is a mixture of faith healing and scientific techniques. She isn't sure why sometimes it works so well and sometimes it doesn't but she does believe that she's seen miracles.

'Sometimes it can be an instant cure but I don't claim to be a healer. I'm just a channel for the light or the energy that heals people. It's usually their faith that makes them better. They're thinking that I'm doing it but it's not me, I'm just a channel and helping to put their energy on that pathway.'

Some of her most dramatic successes have come with couples who were unable to have children.

'I was associated with Foresight, who are the pre-conception care people. They help people who have problems getting pregnant and I used to put them on nutritional programmes and also do some reflexology for them. It's usually the women who come and not the men but on one particular occasion a couple came and I gave her some reflexology. Then her partner said he had a pain in his groin. So I spent a minute pressing his reflexes in his feet, after which the couple left. They were booked in for another appointment the following month, but he rang to cancel because they thought she was pregnant. It seems he'd had a blockage in his tubes, which must have moved on when I showed him where the reflex was.

'There are all sorts of miracle cures that you wouldn't expect. I once treated a lady who had arthritis in her jaw and it was really painful to eat and speak and when I put my hands on her jaw she burst into tears. I thought she was in pain, but she told me that the pain had just melted away when I touched her. She came to see me regularly from Ireland, and in fact her husband was so impressed that he then trained as a reflexologist as well.

Joan takes great satisfaction in the help she can give people through the reflexology. She remembers one little girl in particular whose hip hadn't developed properly as a baby. 'She was missing a hook of bone so her legs were not aligned properly. She was waiting until she was big enough to have a bone graft, but in the meantime she couldn't run, skip or hop. There's not much to work on with a child's feet so I put my hands over the child's hip. Each time I did it, she commented that her hip was getting warm. After four months, when she had an X-ray, the surgeons were astonished to see that the bone had grown back and she wouldn't need the operation. She went on to join a ballet class and did gymnastics and had a normal life.' However, there is no guarantee, and Joan never claims to be able to cure people, only that she will do her best to help.

After Joan's parents died in 1987 she was left their house and, with a little more financial security, she was able to give up her work as a laboratory technician to concentrate on reflexology. These experiences helped her enormously with her own family. As she got older she often thought about where these beliefs or powers might have come from. Her parents weren't religious but she did have an aunt who used to have certain psychic tendencies.

'I was very close to my mother's sister, Elsie. Her husband Tom had died when she was forty, and she strongly believed that he was looking after her. She avoided some awful accidents and she would say, "Tom was looking after me." Joan thinks that she had some kind of psychic bond with her aunt. She remembers times when she had a feeling that she needed to see her, she'd go and visit her and find out that something was wrong.

'Elsie died on Christmas Day. I saw her on

Christmas Eve and the following day while I was in the middle of cooking the Christmas dinner, I had a strong feeling that I had to visit her. I left the dinner to my children and went straight over to her, so I was with her when she died.'

This kind of psychic bond is something that Joan has found herself looking out for in the younger members of her family.

'Billy's mum used to be very psychic as a child,' she says. 'She picked up a lot of traffic accidents in Stockport and she became quite distressed. She used to travel to school by bus, but she was so nervous that we moved her to the Catholic school at the end of the road. She is sensitive. She calls herself an "empath". She is very empathetic. She thinks Billy's psychic in that he can read all of her thoughts. She can't fool him! He picks up people's vibes and he'll decide who he does and doesn't like before they've even said a word.'

But she doesn't think Billy's the only one of the younger generation who's inherited the family gift. Another grandchild had his own problems but also his own special qualities.

'My son's son Jack is a bit psychic,' she says. 'He knows where you've hidden the Christmas presents and things like that!'

Perhaps, though, it was Jack's sheer willpower

that was more impressive than any psychic powers he might have. He suffered a serious illness and was confined to a wheelchair for over a year with a rare neurological problem. But when he was chosen to be a mascot for Manchester United in Europe, he was determined to walk onto the pitch. And he did. He was on his feet all day, and he's not used the wheelchair since.

Joan thinks that another grandson, James, is also unusually sensitive. He could run his hands over a pregnant cat and tell you how many kittens there were, what colours they were and what sex they were. And he was always right. 'When I asked him how he could do that, he told me I didn't relax enough. He even knew where acupuncture points were when he was about three. I think if you're that sensitive you can see light coming out of acupuncture points. One of the most astonishing things he's done though, is when I trapped his finger in the car door and he went screaming round the garden and when we got him in the car to take him home he asked us all to be quiet so he could concentrate. When he got home he got pebbles he'd collected off the beach, made a circle, put his finger in the circle and there wasn't a mark on that finger after that.'

* * *

87

Joan has seen many balls of light during her life, and she strongly believes that these are spirits. She believes, as well, that the orbs that can often be seen on photographs are also spirits, rather than just tricks of photography. Was the ball of light Billy's spirit or was it, as Glennyce Eckersley believes, his Guardian Angel? Joan isn't sure, but she has always thought of balls of light as spirits.

'They like to come to weddings and christenings, occasions of great spiritual meaning. There was even one at my seventieth birthday party.'

Although she sees these balls of light frequently, Joan says that, unlike her grandson Billy, she's never actually seen an angel. Since his experience in hospital Billy has become fascinated with angels, because he says they can heal anything. However, it's still Joan who is the family's greatest exponent of the idea that there is a greater energy in the universe, whatever form that might take. As well as her three children and eight grandchildren she now has three great-grandchildren and she tries to do everything she can for all of them.

'I have to work hard sometimes, with prayer,' she says.

The time when Billy was in the hospital and so ill was particularly frightening, but ever since that day in the delivery room Joan has felt that she has a special connection with Billy. If he was born to help other people then she was there to help him. As far as he is concerned, Grandma is his guardian angel. Joan thinks he says that because when he was little, if he was frightened, she'd cuddle him and say 'Grandma's got you, you're safe.'

'So I think he got the idea that Angels and grandmas work together,' she says.

RICHARD CHATWIN

If we are unlucky, many of us find ourselves in situations of great danger at some point in our lives. For some the situation is a matter of chance, like a car crash or an unprovoked attack. But for others, the very nature of their jobs puts them in the path of danger every day. Being a soldier is one such job. Richard Chatwin's story is an astonishing tale of a life saved in the midst of battle. If he had not stopped and listened, everything could have been very different.

It was a balmy evening in summer; an evening like so many others that Richard Chatwin had experienced while he served with the British Army in Northern Ireland. It was a normal end to a normal day – normal, that is, until something happened that would change his life forever.

It was 1976, and although the Troubles had reignited after a brief ceasefire, Richard had found his time in Northern Ireland uneventful, if occasionally tense. On this particular evening, Richard and his comrades were conducting a routine patrol down a little lane near Cookstown in the countryside of County Tyrone. There was nothing to make any of them think that anything out of the ordinary was going to happen: they had been involved in this type of manoeuvre dozens of times before.

On patrol that evening were two Land Rovers; Richard was driving the second one. In the back of his vehicle, the rest of his troop, a bunch of good-natured, rowdie Geordies, were telling jokes and looking forward to finishing their job and heading back to base. They'd been told to check the culverts – tunnels that linked the drainage ditches on either side of the road. It seemed an odd task to be given and the soldiers speculated about whether it was just the army trying to keep them occupied. It was hard to see why the IRA would be interested in planting explosives out here in the countryside; normally if there was a genuine threat in the area there would be rumours flying about long before any bombs went off. Nevertheless, they had their orders and they knew what they had to do. They'd practised operations like this time and time again.

There were eight people in each Land Rover and they were undertaking a manoeuvre known as 'rolling roadblocks', which involved one Land Rover driving ahead of the other, stopping to let the men out, and then driving on again for about five or six hundred yards, effectively creating a roadblock between two vehicles while the soldiers checked the culverts and the sides of the road.

That evening, when Richard's troop had left the police station that was their temporary base it had just been starting to get dark. Now it was almost pitch black, so it was slow work but they were used to it. They'd been together now for almost two years since arriving for an eighteen-month tour of Northern Ireland. Richard describes his time in the army as rough and tumble, but he loved it. He was young, and at that point in his life he just wanted to have a good career and enjoy himself.

As they reached a T-junction the Land Rover in front of them slowed down and turned right. On their left Richard could just about make out a copse of trees and the looming shadow of an abandoned house. He prepared to follow the vehicle ahead, ready for the next roadblock when, out of the corner of his eye, he saw a flash coming from the direction of the trees. It was too late to react because, at the same instant, there was the unmistakable rattle of machine-gun fire and the deafening sound of bullets smashing against the bodywork of their vehicle. The Land Rover was designed to be bulletproof but there was no guarantee that it could survive that kind of onslaught. The lights on the two Land Rovers were completely exposed, there was nothing between the vehicles and the trees, which made them an easy target: all the gunmen had to do was to shoot between the lights.

Richard immediately switched off the headlights, but it wasn't enough to prevent the chaos of the ensuing seconds. Seconds that felt like hours to the men stranded in the dark inside their vehicles. The first person to react was Richard's colleague John who began returning fire at the back of the Land Rover. As he did so, Richard instinctively slammed on the brakes, sending his passengers forwards. This could have been a disaster, because as he flew from his seat, John kept on shooting, spraying the inside of the Land Rover with machine-gun fire.

Richard stopped the vehicle, and tried to obey his commanding officer's shouted orders to get out of the Land Rover, but he realised with dismay that his webbing was caught up in the door handle. This left the two of them stuck in the cab as gunfire roared around them, helpless either to return fire or find a place of safety. They just had to hope that no bullets would come through the windows or the bodywork.

Finally Richard managed to free himself and the two soldiers were able to get out. Safely under cover, Richard's commanding officer immediately began shooting towards the copse. Richard had been trained for exactly this type of skirmish, and yet the reality of the noise and the chaos of a real gun battle is always a shock. There was no way to know what was happening with the Land Rover ahead of them. There were bullets flying all around and Richard had no idea if any of his comrades had been hit. He was terrified and yet the months of training made his actions instinctive: he reached back into the Land Rover to get his gun from the gun rack.

Suddenly, in the midst of all the action and noise, he heard a voice saying calmly, 'Stop.'

It wasn't the first time he'd heard the voice. It was a male voice, very soft, but at the same time very commanding in an accent and timbre quite unlike his comrades, and Richard found, despite the urgency of the situation, that he couldn't help but obey. For little more than a heartbeat, in the middle of the firefight, he became completely still. It was a decision that would save his life.

Richard had first heard the voice that was to save his life when he was just a child growing up in the West Midlands. He was raised in the same old house where his grandfather and then his father had grown up. It wasn't a frightening place but it was the kind of house that was full of creaks and strange noises at night. There was also an unusual atmosphere about the house, something that you couldn't quite put your finger on, and some family members reported seeing ghosts or other strange spirits. Richard's experience of the forces alive in his house was aural, not visual: he used to hear a voice at exactly the same location every time.

'I must have been about eight or nine the first time I heard it,' he says. 'Whenever I walked towards the front door or went upstairs I'd hear the voice.

All I ever heard was my name being called, so I'd turn around and go back in the house as you do when you think that somebody's calling you. And I knew the voice couldn't belong to any of my family – it had quite a posh accent. No one I knew spoke like that.'

Every time he'd go back inside and look around, wide-eyed, to see who'd called him but there was never anyone there. He couldn't imagine what the voice might want. He never heard anything else except his name but somehow the tone was impossible to resist. It was as though it was speaking directly to him. And it was the very same soft, commanding voice that he heard in the middle of the gun battle years later, so different from the way everybody else in the neighbourhood or in his house spoke.

The West Midlands isn't an area where people are prone to flights of fancy. His family's friends and neighbours were sensible, practical people. Richard had been brought up to be very religious. 'My mum was an Irish Catholic – her mother brought up four girls and one boy. The four girls she put into a convent in Southern Ireland for the nuns to bring up. Then my mum moved to the UK during the war.'

When Richard was just ten years old, his father

died of lung cancer. His father was laid out in the living room after he died, just like his own father before him.

After her husband passed away, Richard's mother was haunted by a strange and frightening apparition. She would hear her husband coming in from his nightshift, going into the kitchen, then eventually coming upstairs and getting into bed. She even felt the bed dip, but there was no one there.

It turns out that it wasn't just his mother that experienced unnerving visits from beyond the grave. Only recently, Richard's sisters told him that as children they'd seen a little girl dressed in a white communion dress in their bedroom.

In this kind of environment the fact that Richard kept hearing his name being called didn't seem that strange. When he talked to his mother about it, she put it down to the house being haunted because both his father and grandfather had died there.

After the death of his father things were very hard for Richard, his brother and his three sisters. His mother didn't have much money and they struggled to make ends meet. But despite everything, he has fond memories of his childhood. It was fun growing up in a big family and the two brothers and three sisters all looked out for each other. His mother's faith became much stronger after her husband died, and she did everything she could to shield them from their poverty and to try and make up for the fact that their dad wasn't around any more.

Richard struggled at school, but from a young age he loved everything to do with the army, so it was a natural progression for him to move from the junior cadets to signing up properly when he was old enough. By the time his unit was on a tour of duty in Northern Ireland in 1976, Richard had already completed tours in Canada and Germany.

It may be that the strong connection to faith, and belief in forces greater than our own, meant that Richard's family were receptive to the spirit world. It also meant that later, when the voice spoke to Richard during the gunfight, he was more inclined to listen to it, and follow what it told him to do.

It could only have been for a fraction of a second that Richard froze after hearing the word 'stop'. The bullets were still flying past. He was standing by the open door of the Land Rover. Between him and the gunmen his only protection was the flak jacket that he was wearing and the bulletproof coating of the vehicle. With the lights of the vehicle off it was almost pitch black. The only source of illumination was the flash of the gunmen's muzzles and the faint sprinkle of stars between the clouds. As he paused there was a different sound from the bullet fire. One of the bullets, instead of ricocheting off the bodywork of the vehicle, had come straight through. As Richard looked at the hole it had made he gasped. It was directly in line with where he would have been leaning in through the door to get his rifle, if the voice hadn't told him to stop. If he'd ignored the voice and reached in to grab his firearm then the sleeve holes of his flak jacket would have virtually been in line with the path of the bullet. It would have gone straight through the sleeve-hole and into his chest.

By now almost everybody was out of the Land Rover and taking up positions all around him, crouching down or leaning over the body of the vehicle to return fire. In all the panic, Richard didn't fully appreciate how miraculous his escape had been. That came much later, once the noise and confusion and terror had died down.

Richard's escape wasn't the only miracle that night. There were bullets flying everywhere but no one was hit. Even when bullets had been flying around the inside of the Land Rover, everyone remained safe. One soldier had leapt out to return fire and his rifle had been shot out of his hands, but incredibly he had escaped injury. The soldiers from the second Land Rover ran back to help their comrades through a hail of bullets, yet not one of them was touched. Even the members of the IRA who were on the receiving end of the soldiers' retaliation escaped unscathed. The Land Rover was testament to just how close they had been to death: it was completely riddled with bullets, and the radio had been shot out. It was a night of miracles. Could there have been an angelic presence protecting everyone from the folly of war that warm summer's evening?

The adrenalin lasted well into the night as the soldiers tried to clear up the mess and establish exactly what had happened. They managed to make contact with the nearest satellite base to call in support and soon the area was being searched by helicopter, but they couldn't find anything. No bodies, and no injured men.

But there was one more nasty surprise for them. When they checked the area where the vehicle had come to a halt they found a two hundred-pound bomb underneath the road, hidden in a culvert. Apparently the UDR [local security forces, the Ulster Defence Regiment] had been using that spot as a rest stop, and the IRA had decided to destroy it.

By the time they'd called in bomb disposal experts, secured the area and cleared up, it was well into the night. Richard's troop didn't get back to base until the next morning and the experience that they'd been through hadn't yet sunk in. Richard just wanted to go to sleep. There was no time to go over what had happened or to think about the strange voice. It didn't even really occur to him that he was lucky to be alive. Everything had happened too fast to appreciate. When he woke up the next day, though, he felt very different.

'I was incredibly happy to be alive. It was like I was on a high. When I went outside, the colours were sharper, and everything seemed a lot brighter. It was a very strong feeling of well-being. It was as though I was up there in the clouds.'

It was only then that he started to think about the voice that had saved his life. For the first time he even tried to communicate with it, but he got no reply.

Richard had no idea whose voice it could be. The voice had a posh English accent, so it couldn't have been any of the soldiers. They all had strong Geordie accents. It wasn't the voice of any of his friends or family, either. He'd been brought up in the West Midlands and most of the people he knew had Black Country accents. His mother's side of the family were all Irish and the voice didn't sound like them either.

The voice wasn't like anybody he knew. So who on earth could it be? He couldn't explain what had happened or who the voice belonged to, but the incident changed his life. Nonetheless, he didn't tell anybody what had happened to him.

'I felt euphoric for a couple of days and then it slowly wore off. The next time we went out we just carried on and the incident was basically forgotten about. I couldn't mention something like that because I'd have got the mickey ripped out of me. They were a bunch of Geordies. You couldn't tell them anything like that.'

Richard wanted to tell somebody about what had happened. He needed to make sense of it to himself but he was scared of the consequences if he did. So it wasn't until he was home on leave that he told his girlfriend, his brother and his sisters.

Sadly for Richard, though he loved being in the army, shortly after the incident in Northern Ireland he received terrible news. He'd known for a long time that his mother had a weak heart but it was still a shock to be told that she had just two weeks to live. He'd already pulled out of Ireland twice because of his mother's health, and this time, though the army was sympathetic, they gave him a compassionate discharge and told him that he could always re-apply later. His record of service should stand him in good stead.

He went back home to the West Midlands to be near his mother but she was stronger than anyone had thought. She lived for another two years. It was a great relief for the whole family but it did mean that Richard put off his return to the armed forces. Meanwhile, after her brush with death, Richard's mother became increasingly interested in spiritualism and began consulting mediums. Richard tended not to take much notice of his mother's preoccupation with the spirit world. However, there was one incident that Richard can't explain to this day. His mother was having a consultation with a medium one afternoon, and Richard was leaving the house to carry out some errands, but just as he was heading out the front door, on the same spot where he had heard that strange voice as a child, he heard his name being called. Returning to the kitchen he asked his mother what she wanted, but she hadn't spoken his name. However, it transpired that he had been called back for a reason: his mother's medium had a message for him. She told him that he was going to get married, but the woman he would wed was not the right one for him. However, she said reassuringly, all would turn out well in the end.

Is it possible that the spirit he believes protected him on that violent day in 1976 wanted to warn him of the difficult years ahead, and to let him know that he would come through the experience eventually?

Richard was already thinking of proposing to his girlfriend and the prophecy didn't put him off. He loved his girlfriend and thought that the medium was wrong. So, in spite of the warning, he and his girlfriend soon married. Not long afterwards they were overjoyed when their baby daughter, Samantha, was born. It was the most exciting, life-changing thing that had ever happened to him but it was also the start of new problems. Sadly, his mother did not live long enough to see her new grandchild, and Richard's happiness at becoming a dad was tempered by the grief he felt when his mother passed away. Added to these new and raw emotions, the responsibility of being a father weighed heavily on him and he was determined to get a good job to support his daughter – unfortunately he had left it too late to rejoin the army.

Instead he got a job as a van driver. The couple were happy for a while but things rapidly went downhill. Although he adored his newborn daughter the relationship wasn't working and, after just eighteen months of marriage, Richard and his wife split up. If that wasn't bad enough, he lost contact with his daughter. And so began a very difficult time in his life as he was plunged into depression.

After losing Samantha Richard became clinically depressed. He was prescribed antidepressants but it was hard to tell whether they were helping. His whole life appeared to have fallen apart.

'I spent four years on antidepressants, and during that time I lost my job and really hit rock bottom.'

He wasn't eating properly or looking after himself. He was also becoming harder for his friends and family to deal with. They wanted to help him but they were growing increasingly exasperated by his inability to help himself.

It was difficult to see how he would ever be able to snap out of it. One day, though, the fog of depression lifted as suddenly as it had arrived. He woke up after a seemingly innocuous dream where he looked out of the window and saw a friend of his arrive to take him for a drive. But when he turned around to go to the door, he woke up and realised he was still in bed. Could this have been a message that he was not alone? Richard says that from that moment on he didn't touch another tablet. It wasn't a sensible way to deal with antidepressants but it seemed to work for him. He gradually began to recover. What he needed most was a new start and, fortunately for him, that was just around the corner. One sister had been living abroad, and when she came back from South Africa, she moved to Telford and brought Richard to live there with her. The new surroundings invigorated him and he soon found a job and started putting his life back together.

And that included meeting Angela. Angela already had a daughter, Zoe, and together they had another child, Kieran. Sadly, the marriage didn't last, but both children stayed with Richard and he and his children were happy.

The only cloud was the fact that he still had no idea where his oldest daughter Samantha was. Then, almost twenty-five years after his first wife left him, he received a letter.

'Samantha's grandmother wrote to tell me that Samantha was getting married and would I like to get in touch.'

Suddenly Richard remembered what the medium had told him. Twenty-five years seems a very long time to wait for it all to work out in the end, but he'd never stopped hoping that he would see his eldest daughter again.

Richard and Samantha exchanged emails to begin

with, but finally they arranged to meet. Richard had been waiting for this moment for years but when the time came he couldn't deal with the turmoil he was feeling, and in the days leading up to their first meeting, he worried what Samantha would think of him, agonising over the thought that this might be the only time that they would ever meet.

While he was waiting to meet his daughter for the first time in twenty-five years, he found himself overcome with emotion. He hadn't seen Samantha since she was a toddler and he worried that she would be bitter or angry with him. He just prayed that he wouldn't be a disappointment to the daughter he longed to see so much. As he stood outside the pub, silently praying that everything would turn out all right, he looked up and suddenly there she was. His little girl, grown into a lovely woman, the spitting image of her mother. And the two have been close ever since, so whether it was his Guardian Angel, or one of the spirits that seemed to haunt his family home, the message that they had sent all those years ago had finally come true.

After his miraculous escape in Northern Ireland Richard Chatwin had been through a lot. He had only ever wanted a normal family life and he had struggled to cope when it was taken away from him. Despite a period of severe depression, after leaving the army he felt like he'd become a different person. The day he heard the voice say 'stop' something inside him was different.

'While I was in the army my life didn't appear to change that much. But I became a more giving person after I left the army. I started donating money to charity, especially children's charities.'

He firmly believes that if he needs help badly enough that it will come. He now runs his own business as a plastics fabricator. Like almost all small business owners he's had times when work has been scarce, but something has always turned up to help him get by. He started repairing computers to earn a bit of extra money and he's found that, very often, somebody will offer him some work if he needs it.

'I've never asked anybody for anything. If I run out of money now, something always turns up. I feel lucky.'

Whether it is from a Guardian Angel or a spiritual guide, Richard believes that there is support for everyone, and that everyone's life is mapped out for them from the day they are born. Even in the dark years after his first wife left with his daughter, he is sure now that there was a presence looking after him then, although at the time he was too depressed to allow the possibility of a benign, loving presence into his life.

Richard has not heard that voice since it called him into the kitchen all those years ago. 'If ever I go back to where I used to live I have a strong feeling that I have to stop outside. Because that's where I used to hear the voice.'

The voice has never been explained. It's just one of many mysteries that have been a part of his life since his childhood. Some of them have only recently come to light, like the story about the ghostly child that his sisters saw. Since then the family have done some research to see if there was a young child who died there, but so far there is no explanation for her appearance there. Richard has no idea whether the child is connected in any way to the voice that he used to hear.

Even more strangely a ghostly presence seems to have followed him to his new home in Telford.

'I'm sure there used to be a little girl living in this house. My ex-wife used to like to sleep with her arms out of the bed, and one night she woke up screaming because she said she felt somebody holding her hand. I also have felt something in the bedroom. For example, I used to have a normal-size bed and, being quite tall, my feet would hang off the bottom. And

I felt as though somebody was walking across the bottom of the bed and brushing against my feet.'

It's as though something from the mysterious old house where he grew up follows him wherever he goes. But if there is a supernatural presence in Richard's life it seems to be a benign one, as the positive elements have outweighed the negative. It's now six years since he was reunited with his oldest daughter, Samantha. His other children are both attending, or about to attend, university. His life has, as the medium promised, turned out all right and, to add to his joy, he has just become a grandfather for the first time. But Richard can't forget that, without that commanding 'stop' all those years ago, none of his children would have existed and that baby would never have been born.

LALLA DUTT

There are times in life when you know you are
on the wrong path, but it's hard to find your way
back to where you need to be. Some of us are
lucky enough to have an angel guide us gently back
in the right direction. And that is what happened
to Lalla Dutt.

Lalla Dutt knew that working as a sales assistant wasn't the worst job in the world. Her job at the trendy Whistles store in Covent Garden paid her bills and was interesting, up to a point. Clothes had always been her passion and she really enjoyed helping customers find outfits that made them look and feel good. But, as she often told herself, it was only temporary. Eventually she would start the career of her dreams, in fashion journalism.

Immediately after leaving London University Lalla had done very well, having articles published in numerous national magazines and newspapers. But the recession of the late 1980s and early 1990s had hit the media hard. As freelance work dried up Lalla went from being part-time at Whistles to full-time. A year went by, then two, and after three years struggling to find a way into the industry she was so passionate about, she started to wonder what she was doing with her life. Would she work in retail for ever? Her dream hadn't died but it was becoming harder to maintain her self-belief in the face of rejection letters and lack of response from editors. It felt like she'd need a miracle to break into the career she'd wanted to follow ever since she was a young girl.

Lalla, who was a very creative child, had always known that she wanted to work in journalism and desperately wanted to be editor of *Vogue*, the most influential fashion magazine in the world. When she was about eight or nine she used to write to Beatrix Miller, then editor of *Vogue*, sending in stories and illustrating the envelopes so that they were works of art in themselves. The busy editor saw Lalla's potential and wrote back to her.

'Beatrix Miller was very kind and told me there were two ways I could fulfil my dream, and that was either by doing a journalism degree or entering the *Vogue* Talent Contest. Of course, I was determined to enter the contest as soon as I was old enough.'

The *Vogue* Talent Contest, a competition for writers, is still running to this day, over sixty years since it was first conceived and is one of the most prestigious writing competitions around – many famous journalists, authors and even playwrights launched their career by winning the competition. It currently offers a prize of £1,000 plus a month's paid work experience at *Vogue*. It goes without saying that even getting into the final of this competition is a tremendous step up for a young journalist wanting to break into this extremely competitive field.

Lalla wasn't a very outgoing teenager but she was aware of her strengths and weaknesses and she knew that she was a good writer. It was difficult to be patient, but with her characteristic single mindedness, Lalla filled the years before she was old enough to enter by honing her craft. As soon as her seventeenth birthday arrived she sent in an article to the competition.

To her delight, Lalla received a letter telling her that she'd reached the next stage of the competition, even though she was one of the youngest entrants.

'I was a finalist and at that time you got taken along to a big lunch at the Conde Nast offices [Conde Nast is the publisher of *Vogue*] and they chose the winner on the basis of how you behave. That year there was no winner, we were all finalists.'

It was a major boost to her ambitions. Afterwards Lalla undertook a degree in English literature at London University, and with the grades she received, and the encouragement of her tutors, she had good grounds for being confident that a successful career in the media awaited her. After she left university she sent out hundreds of letters with pitches for articles to magazines around the country.

To supplement her income, Lalla took a job as

a sales assistant at Whistles. It wasn't exactly what she wanted to do but she had to pay her rent and at least it was a connection to the industry that she loved so much. The problem was that the time she spent in the shop made it harder for her to find time to write. When she came home in the evening she was tired and she often found herself working at the weekends. She was still writing, but not as much as she had been before.

Soon the journalism side of her life started to dwindle, although it never went away. Lalla hadn't given up her dream of editing *Vogue*, even if the recession was making it harder to find work in journalism. It was difficult for Lalla to remain upbeat about her chances of making it as a writer. While writing was still important to her, it had become more of an outlet for her thoughts and feelings, rather than something she could include in her portfolio with a view to publication.

Lalla's life wasn't so bad but she knew she was capable of so much more. Working in the shop gave her very few opportunities for creativity. She felt stifled and, although she liked the other staff, she spent much of her time working by herself. One particularly hard Monday, she spent a long time with a difficult customer who eventually left without buying anything. Lalla felt uncharacteristically despondent after the customer left, so she took an early lunch break to cheer herself up, and also to buy the *Guardian*, which advertised media jobs on a Monday, to see if there were any jobs she could apply for.

'I went to the covered area of Covent Garden market, near Drury Lane, where there was a little café that I liked to go to,' she recalls. 'It was a lovely place. They displayed their cakes beautifully in the window and even had a pair of Victorian gloves draped on one side. I thought I'd sit down with a coffee for twenty minutes and look through the paper to see if there were any jobs that would suit me.'

To her annoyance she found that the section with the media jobs in it wasn't inside her paper. Any other day it wouldn't have upset her that much, but on that day, when she was feeling so despondent and hopeless, it felt like just one more thing that had gone wrong. But rather than going to exchange the paper, she decided to calm down and read.

The café was a friendly sort of place. Despite being in the heart of London many of the people who came in knew each other.

'I clearly remember the scene: there was a woman at the counter talking very loudly, two girls and a boy behind the counter, and various customers all chatting. It was nice and companionable, not too noisy, not too quiet.'

But suddenly the atmosphere changed.

'This guy came in and immediately the room seemed to go quiet. He wasn't amazingly handsome. He wasn't amazingly tall. He was just extremely arresting. He wasn't like anybody else there. There was something about him that made everyone stop. It sounds ridiculous but it was almost as if he was glowing. There was nothing forced with him, it was very fluid and quite compelling. Covent Garden's a very busy area and to see somebody walking through it with that calm and serenity, I just thought, wow, lucky him.'

For a few moments everyone in the café seemed to be frozen. Everyone was looking at the man but he didn't take any notice. He just sat down quietly. It was as though he wasn't aware of being the centre of attention.

'Then everything started up again as it was before,' Lalla remembers. 'I can't tell you how long it was quiet for. I was just aware that a little bell went, the man came into the café and it all went quiet, and then all at once it went back to normal.'

Lalla went back to reading her paper, trying not to think about the fact that she had to go back to work soon. She didn't notice the man again until she realised that he was standing by her table holding a paper. His sudden appearance startled her. She forgot the feeling of peace she'd had when he'd first walked in.

'I'm ashamed to say I felt disgruntled when I saw him standing over me. He gave me the paper and said, "I think you might want this." It was the *Media Guardian*. At first I thought he must have realised I'd been looking for it, but he hadn't even been in the café when I'd arrived. Then I thought it was quite sweet of him. I thanked him. But, and I rue this to this day, I didn't say it particularly politely or with much grace. Then he said, "You might want to look on page thirty-five" and he smiled and left. And I didn't smile back.'

Lalla was confused. She didn't know how the mysterious stranger knew what she'd been looking for, or why he thought she would be interested in a particular page. She was a little embarrassed, too. It was strange to find that somebody that she didn't know was able to tell what she was thinking. After he left the café she didn't open the paper immediately.

'I waited until he'd gone before I looked because I thought, I didn't want to give him the satisfaction if he'd been making fun of me but I was curious, so I had a look as soon as he left.

There were lots of jobs on page 35 but, for some reason, one of them caught her eye. It was an advert for a copywriter for Freemans catalogue. Working for a mail-order company wasn't something that Lalla had considered before, but the job looked good so she sent her application off straight away.'

At the time she didn't think there was anything particularly significant about her strange encounter. It was odd, certainly, but she didn't think it would change her life. When she received a letter from Freemans not long afterwards, informing her that she'd been unsuccessful in her application, she wasn't surprised, just a little disappointed. But that wasn't the end of the story.

'I got a call when I was home one day saying, "You haven't been successful for this job" and I thought, "Thanks a lot. I know. I got the letter."'

But there was more. Her CV made the people at Freemans think that she was over-qualified for a copywriting job. But they had another job they thought might suit her better. They asked her to go in for a chat about being the editor for their in-house publication. And when they mentioned the salary, Lalla couldn't believe it. It was a lot more than she was earning at Whistles.

She went in for an interview, feeling very

nervous, but it was surprisingly easy. It was as though they'd already decided that she was the right person for the job. She had exactly the qualities they were looking for. All Lalla needed to do was confirm their expectations.

Even then it didn't seem as though something miraculous had happened. For a long time Lalla was too busy to think about that fateful day in the café, because once she'd started, Freemans also gave her some PR work for the company, which she really enjoyed. And it was in PR that her career progressed. Lalla eventually left Freemans, having been courted by various different companies.

By the late 1990s, Lalla was enjoying her chosen profession too much to spend much time thinking about how she'd reached this point in her life. However, as time went by, her thoughts turned back to the stranger in the café. Had he really given her a gentle push down the road she was travelling? And if so, who was he?

It was evitable that Lalla would start thinking more deeply about that mysterious stranger whose act of kindness had such a huge effect on her life. Lalla's career may have involved the fun and froth of fashion PR, but she'd been brought up to believe that life isn't all about material wealth and possessions, that there's more to the world than meets the eye.

Lalla comes from a very normal, suburban background. Her father worked in advertising and she and her brother grew up in Dollis Hill, north-west London. Her parents raised her to be down to earth and to believe that hard work was the secret to success.

But when she thinks back on the life of her family she is struck by the extraordinary sequence of coincidences and strokes of fortune that led her to being where she is today. Her mother grew up in Kerala in south India, where she was brought up as a Syrian orthodox Christian, but she met Lalla's father in England.

'My mother was supposed to get married in India but she didn't want to. Instead, as my uncle was coming here to study my mum came with him and here she met my father. She came from a very religious background, one of her brothers is a priest, but my father had no religion and we weren't brought up religiously. We weren't taken to church or anything. It was a very free existence.'

Lalla's father didn't press any spiritual beliefs on his children. They were brought up to believe in good manners and kindness but not in any type of creed. However, his family line includes some of the most significant figures of their age in the sub-continent. They were people who would have had no difficulty in believing in angels.

'My father's side of the family is very interesting. My great-grandfather was a poet and his brother was a philosopher called Sri Aurabindo Ghosh. He started an ashram in south India with a French nun called The Mother. He advised Gandhi during the partition of India. He meditated and for many years took a vow of silence. When he died he was laid out in state.'

Sri Aurabindo Ghosh and his brother, Lalla's great-grandfather, were sent to England to be educated when they were children. Their father was an ardent anglophile who believed that it would be better for them to become as British as possible.

'The two brothers were told by their father that he didn't want them to have anything to do with India,' says Lalla. 'So my great-grandfather became a proper Englishman. He and his brother both went to St Paul's and Oxford. My great-grandfather was a poet and an artist and he wrote lots of books. But my great-uncle wanted to find his own path and went back to India.'

Back in India, Lalla's great-uncle became very

involved in the struggle against the British Empire. He learned more about his own country's philosophy and combined it with what he'd studied in Oxford. As a result, his beliefs were a mixture of Western philosophy and Christianity that he combined with his Hindu roots.

Sri Aurabindo Ghosh was a firm believer in angelic intervention. He claimed that he, too, had been saved by angels. One of his essays describes an incident in his early twenties after his return to India when he was riding in a horse carriage. The carriage almost crashed but the accident was averted by what he described as a 'being of light'. He wrote a poem about it later.

Above my head a mighty head was seen,
A face with the calm of immortality
And an omnipotent gaze that held the scene
In the vast circle of its sovereignty.
His hair was mingled with the sun and breeze;
The world was in His heart and He was I:
I housed in me the Everlasting's peace,
The strength of One whose substance cannot die.'

In India Sri Aurabindo Ghosh is still revered as a great man.

'When he died he had stamps dedicated to him

in India. In London there's still an organisation on Finchley Road that reads his works. I often think that perhaps he was an angel. There were loads of different interventions that saved his life. Perhaps I and my brother wouldn't be here had it not been for the intervention of angels, or fate, or a higher being, or whatever you want to call it.'

So perhaps it's the presence of Sri Aurabindo Ghosh in her family tree that makes Lalla so receptive to the idea of angels.

Although not raised in a strictly conventional sense, her mother had always taught her to be kind and to treat people well.

'She's very calm, very kind and very wise,' Lalla explains. 'She's one of eight and she was born in abject poverty in Kerala. She may not have had a formal education, but she has a knowledge above most people's. If people treat her badly she doesn't feel that she should treat them badly in return. There is no sense of vengeance in her. She's an endless well of hope and charity.'

A couple of years before her mysterious encounter in the café Lalla's father died. Understandably it had a big impact on her life.

'It was a shock when my father passed away,' she admits. 'He had a heart attack and it was very sudden. I still feel his presence, however, and I think he will always be looking out for me because we were very close.'

Despite this Lalla still remembers the most important lesson she learnt from her parents. She believes that life helps those who help themselves.

'I do think that my dad looks out for me,' she confirms. 'But I don't think he can change what I do or how I do it. You have to take advantage of the opportunities that come your way. If an angel is directing you down a certain path, it's up to you to take that road, and to make the most of what you find there.'

It wasn't until a few years after her encounter in the café that Lalla started to wonder what was behind it. It was partly her increasing success and the consciousness of how fragile that success can be that turned her mind back to the mysterious man. She grew increasingly convinced that there are things that cannot be explained by science, and became fascinated by the idea that there might be spirits, angels or some sort of higher power existing in tandem with our own, more prosaic, world.

Even then, though, the word 'angel' didn't come into her thoughts. It was hard for her to believe that somebody would come down from heaven just to help her.

'I didn't think of it as an angelic experience but I did think that there must be a good soul somewhere around that wanted to help someone. I didn't feel that he was meant especially for me. It might have been anybody. If I'd taken my lunch two hours later he might have come in and helped them. I believe in a higher source but I don't believe it engineers what happens in this world. I just felt like I was at the right place at the right time. It was only when somebody asked me if I'd ever had an angelic experience that I thought that maybe I had.'

But she does believe that that day changed her life. She doesn't know what would have happened if she hadn't turned to page 35 of the job section but she does know that her life is completely different from before.

'It set me back on the path that I was always supposed to be on. Three years after seeing the angel I was taken on by a PR company and three months after that I became a board director.'

The day that Lalla met her 'angel' changed her life and, although she's reluctant to rely too much on higher forces to save her in times of need, she is adamant that something very special happened that day.

It has been suggested to her that perhaps the man in the café was just an ordinary man, that there was a physical chemistry between them, rather than anything spiritual. Lalla rejects this interpretation. Despite the fact that she thought he was handsome she insists that he really wasn't her type.

Since that day there have been occasions when Lalla could have done with her Guardian Angel again. However, it's never occurred to her that she should ask for him to come back.

'If I'm lucky enough to see him again then I will be very happy, but I won't expect to.'

For Lalla the most important part of the experience was the sense that there might be something more to the universe than what exists on this material plane. With her drive and commitment she would have got a good job eventually but she believes that her experience proves that there is something else out there, something that is perhaps too great for us to know, but which casts a benign eye over us and gently places us back on the right path when we have been drifting from it.

Lalla's day-to-day life pulls her in two directions: she describes herself as a dreamer and yet she's been very successful in a career that requires a healthy dose of cynicism. Similarly, when it comes to more spiritual matters, she's also torn: on an intellectual level she thinks that the world is too corrupt for there to be a higher power and yet emotionally and spiritually she believes in angels.

'If you want to look for angels you'll find one,' she says. 'I'd love to think that the man in the café was my angel!'

LEE DIN

Life takes people in many different directions, and Lee Din is no exception. From a difficult childhood in Salford, which was well documented in the popular film *East is East*, he became a very successful hairdresser and make-up artist. He'd always felt a presence helping and protecting him throughout his life, but did his Guardian Angel guide him back home, at a time when he really needed to be there? Here is Lee's fascinating story.

'You've got a tumour in your neck, what are you going to do about it?' The voice was so loud, urgent and sudden that Lee Din woke up with a start and sat bolt upright. It sounded like someone was yelling directly in his ear. He sat there in the dark room, shaking, for several seconds. There was nobody there who could have spoken to him but this wasn't just a voice in his head. It was a shout, almost a scream. It had a strong Manchester accent, just like his, but it didn't sound like anybody he knew.

Lee put his hand to his neck and felt the slight swelling there. He'd noticed it before but hadn't really thought anything of it. Could he have been wrong? He shook his head; he was being ridiculous, he'd had a bad dream that was all.

After sitting up for a few minutes Lee lay down again and tried to get back to sleep, but despite what his logical mind was telling him, he couldn't help worrying.

'It was shocking and terrifying. This voice was screaming at me. I think if I'd felt like it was just in my head I'd have turned over and gone back to sleep. But it felt as though somebody was in the room or right in my ear.'

Lee lay awake in bed worrying. He'd had what he thought was a swollen gland for quite some time, and he'd ignored it. He was too busy to be ill or spare the time it took to see a doctor. His career as a hairdresser, stylist and make-up artist was incredibly successful and he devoted every hour in the day to his chosen profession.

In the end he calmed down. He told himself, against his better judgement, that he'd just had a weird nightmare, and that because he had a bit of a lump on his neck, he must have been subconsciously thinking about it, which is why he'd had the dream. He was sure that his swollen gland was down to stress and tiredness, and there was nothing more to it than that. Despite being very shaken up, he didn't tell anyone what he'd heard, not even his partner Michael, his family or his closest friends.

Lee can admit now what he refused to acknowledge then. 'If someone told me this story, I'd be the first person to say that somebody's trying to tell you something, but I really didn't want to know. I couldn't even tell Michael, even though we always discuss everything. I was in total denial. But I just kept telling myself it was a bad dream.

It wasn't just a dream. The next day at work

Lee felt even more tired than usual, which he put down to his disturbed night. His fatigue didn't go unnoticed, as his colleagues kept asking him if he was okay, but he assured them that he was fine.

After a while, though, as the lump got bigger and he still felt tired, he decided it was time to put his mind at rest by going to see the doctor.

The doctor reassured him that it was a swollen gland, and gave him some medication. With relief, Lee put the experience to the back of his mind and continued with his punishing work schedule. But the lump didn't disappear. Instead it seemed to be growing. Lee couldn't ignore it any longer, so he went back to the doctor, who sent him to the hospital for a check-up.

Even then Lee wasn't particularly worried. He went by himself to the hospital, not thinking that there was anything seriously wrong. He was sure that if there was he would have felt much more ill than he did. But the hospital visit did not go as he had expected. As soon as the doctor had inspected the lump, he was whisked into surgery for a biopsy.

Expecting the worst, Michael and Lee returned to hospital the following week to get the results. But even though they'd tried to prepare themselves, it was still the most frightening thing that they could hear.

'They told me it was a stage four tumour. Stage one is the lowest. Then they told me they'd found another tumour attached to the first one.'

Lee should have been terrified but he felt strangely calm. Rather than panicking he began looking into his options. 'I asked the doctor what my chances were, and when he said sixty–forty in favour of me living, I felt quite calm. I just wanted to get on with it. There was no point panicking and complaining. So I prepared myself for the chemo and, although it was really hard, I never panicked.'

Lee has a strong belief in the afterlife and that gave him a lot of comfort. He's always thought that there is a better world after this one but this was a real test of his faith.

'I couldn't help feeling that, considering every-thing I'd preached about life after death and what I believe, I'd be a bit of a hypocrite if I was the one who started panicking if I thought that I was going to die. I can honestly say I wasn't scared of dying.'

Understandably, though, Michael was scared. In a way it was even harder for him because he didn't feel able to show how he felt. He didn't want to frighten Lee or make it any worse for him.

'We went together for the results and he didn't show me how shocked he was. While I was going through the treatment, he only revealed his worries to our families and friends. He was very, very strong for me. We got through it together, really.'

The first stage of his treatment was chemotherapy. It was a process that, for nine weeks, took over his life.

'I went through three weeks of chemotherapy where I was literally strapped to a machine for twenty-four hours a day, five days a week. I'd have a break for two weeks, then back again for the same thing.'

He'd steeled himself to cope with any kind of pain or discomfort and, because of that, the chemotherapy didn't seem quite as gruelling as he'd expected. It was, however, extremely tiring.

What helped Lee immensely was that he had so many close friends around him in Manchester. He particularly remembers the help he received from TV doctor Chris Steele, of ITV programme *This Morning*, who he'd come to know through his work as a TV make-up artist.

'A week after I started chemo Chris Steele came round and he gave me advice, and good nutritional information about all the honey I should take and the juicing I should do.'

After Chris left, Lee started to think about the different circumstances that had led to him returning to live in Manchester, among people who could help him.

'It seemed that everyone I needed to have around me to get better was here with me in Manchester. I could have been in Florida; I could have been in London where it was an hour's drive to a hospital. It was really weird that when I needed them all these things fell into place. Some of my family live nearby and my friends that I've made over the years, they've all helped me tremendously.'

While recovering from his chemotherapy, Lee started to think more deeply about the voice he'd heard. He'd long believed in the concept of Guardian Angels and it suddenly struck him that the voice was that of his very own angel.

The voice didn't just reaffirm his belief that he had a Guardian Angel, it also confirmed his belief that he'd always been guided and protected, ever since he was a young boy.

Lee's childhood wasn't easy. He was born to a Muslim father and a Catholic mother in Salford in the early 1950s. Right from the start there was tension between the two cultures as his father struggled to maintain his family's Pakistani roots while his children wanted the freedom to choose for themselves how to live their lives. At that time

Salford was almost entirely white and they were surrounded by what their father considered to be excessively liberal influences. Lee didn't meet his two older brothers until he was five because they'd been sent away to be brought up in Pakistan. His father thought that if they lived in Pakistan during their formative years they would be inoculated against the more negative side of Western culture.

'I had two older brothers and when the youngest was about a year old my father asked my mother if he could send them back. She didn't want to let them go but he wanted to send them back to his mother. He convinced her that they were going to go on a three-month holiday and she didn't see them again for five years. In the meantime I was born. So I never knew them. When they came back they couldn't speak the language or anything.'

But in Manchester Lee and his other siblings were exposed to a very different culture, as the new music and fashion of the 1960s started to sweep away old-fashioned, conservative ideas of all kinds. Lee's father wanted them to move to a more overtly 'Asian' area but his mother wouldn't allow it.

'My mum knew that if we moved we would have been totally taken over by the Asian society. Until

141

I was fourteen we were the only Asian family in the school.'

His mum and dad eventually had thirteen children, of which ten survived, and Lee was the third oldest. When he was grown up they all shared a four-bedroomed house and it was a raucous, lively upbringing.

If this story sounds familiar it's because Lee's younger brother Ayub wrote about their upbringing in an autobiographical play, which was later turned into the very successful film *East is East*. The film is a comedy, but Lee remembers a much darker element to his childhood. Lee's dad ran a chip shop and to his customers he seemed like a cheerful, friendly character but there was another side to him.

'If you were a customer in the shop you'd have thought he was wonderful. But he was cruel. My childhood was quite violent, really. My father was very violent and very cruel. I don't think he liked me very much from the day I was born.'

The problems between them became much, much worse when Lee decided that he wanted to be a hairdresser.

'We lived in Salford, one of the roughest areas of Manchester, and our next-door neighbour was a hairdresser and she used to come out smelling of lacquer with her hair in a beehive. I used to think that she was so glamorous. It was the glamour that I was after.'

His father didn't think that hairdressing was a suitable occupation for a boy but Lee was determined to follow his dreams. So when he saw an advertisement for an assistant at a plush salon in the centre of Manchester, Lee applied. He had no experience of hairdressing, and he was only fifteen years old, but somehow his naivety proved to be an advantage and he got the job. Could his angel have been guiding and helping him even then?

Lee's choice of work widened the rift between him and his dad but it also caused arguments between his parents. His mum always supported him but his dad couldn't see that working in a luxury salon could be the start of a successful career.

'It really split the whole family. I just thought that it was something I had to do but my father came to this country in 1932, so he left India when it was still the British Raj. To him barbers were people who worked in the streets. When I became a hairdresser at fifteen he didn't speak to me again until I was twenty-three. If I walked into the house, he walked out.'

In the end Lee's father lost the battle to make his children follow a traditional Pakistani path. All of them, to one degree or another, rejected that aspect of their upbringing. It was Lee, though, who even as a child seemed to represent the strongest rejection of his father's values. This made him a target for his father's violence and there were many times when he felt like he was in real danger. Looking back he believes that, throughout this time, he was protected from the worst of his father's violence by his Guardian Angel.

'There were certain times when he could have been really violent but somebody was always there. Somebody would walk in and he'd have to stop. Or there were times when if I'd been there two minutes earlier I'd have got a battering. There was always something that helped me. I knew that somebody was watching out for me.'

The release of the play and the film version of *East is East* was a highly emotional experience for Lee, but it also helped him to deal with what he'd been through.

'I went to see the play and I didn't think the violence in it would affect me the way it did. My whole body was shaking. So when the film came out I thought that there was no way I could go and see it. When it came out on DVD Michael bought it, and I watched it for the first time. I think it broke my heart all the way through. I cried from the start to the finish. I watched it two or three times and it had the same effect. There's a part in it when the mother runs to the telephone box to speak to the son about the violence of the father, and in real life that son was me, I'm on the other end of the phone saying, "Mum, I can't do anything for you. What do you want me to do?" But watching the movie and seeing that episode from her point of view, seeing what she was going through when she talked to me in the telephone box, it had a totally different effect on me.'

By then Lee was already far removed from the violence and intolerance of his father. He'd moved on, and he thinks it's very possible that this was with the help of some angelic guidance.

At the salon his career went from strength to strength. He also became more interested in spiritual issues, abandoning the extremism that he'd been brought up with but taking the best parts of what he saw in many different religions. He read books about everything from Judaism to witchcraft but in the end none of it was a perfect fit.

'My father was a Muslim, my mother was a Catholic and I went to a Protestant school, but I'd abandoned all organised religion. I just took what I thought was the most relevant for me from each one and tried to live my life with love, respect, understanding and compassion. The father of a friend of mine was a spiritual healer, I chatted to him a lot and I got very involved in a spiritualist church and in that spiritual way of life.'

As his interest in spiritualism grew Lee started exploring other areas of spirituality. He attended a 'spiritual development' group where he says he had a vision of his 'spirit guide'.

'We would all sit in a circle around a medium, who was the conduit through which our spirit guides contacted us. This guy called "Tamjasin" came through for me. He was a Tibetan monk. He was small and thin and had a pointy white beard, like Confucius. He called me "the boy" and then said that because my spiritual level wasn't high enough he couldn't come down to see me unless I raised my level a bit higher.'

Tamjasin on a couple of occasions, including once during his treatment, and his presence filled him with peace and tranquillity.

Lee carried on searching and exploring spiritual ideas, trying to raise his awareness, and when he was still working in his salon, he received a strange prophecy.

'I went to see a clairvoyant in the early 1980s and she told me she could see me surrounded by lights and water. I was living in the centre of Manchester at the time and I thought, "I can't see myself opening a business in Blackpool!"'

A few years later, Lee branched out from hairdressing. He became interested in photography and it seemed natural, as he was doing his clients' hair, to learn about other aspects of styling as well.

Finally Lee started working for a new television programme featuring two unknown presenters. The programme was called *This Morning* and the two presenters were a married couple named Richard Madeley and Judy Finnigan. And then he remembered the prophecy he'd been given more than ten years before. 'I was in Liverpool, on the docks, surrounded by water, under bright lights in the studio.'

In 2001, Lee decided it was time for an adventure. So he and Michael moved to New York. But when they got there, things didn't work out quite as they planned. They arrived in New York in August 2001. They'd expected it to be incredibly exciting and dynamic, and it was, but there was also something wrong. Somehow they both felt uncomfortable.

'Michael was desperate to go to New York but once we got there he said he really didn't want to be there anymore because he felt as if he couldn't breathe.'

It was very strange. After all their plans, and everything they had hoped to achieve there, suddenly Michael felt they should leave. They went and had lunch in the Twin Towers and as they went up in the lift, Lee said, 'My God, if anything happened in this building you wouldn't stand a chance.'

Once again, it seemed that there was some angelic intervention that prevented them from making a seriously wrong decision. Although on this occasion, perhaps it was Michael's angel whispering in his ear, telling him to get out of New York as quickly as they could.

So, instead of staying in New York they went to Florida and, two weeks later, the World Trade Center was destroyed in a horrific and unprecedented act of terrorism; it changed the atmosphere in America completely.

Michael and Lee decided to stay in Florida but, even there, they found a new mood of fear and suspicion. Lee found work in advertising, TV and film but nothing full-time. He felt that his Asian background made him the subject of racism and prejudice. It was while he was in America that he had another vision of his spirit guide.

'There have only been a couple of times when I've felt him around. Once during chemotherapy; the other time during those anxious years while I was in the States. I felt as though someone had put a hand on my head, and then I saw Tamjasin. It was very calming. He didn't smile. He just looked at me with a very reassuring expression.'

Lee had always been interested in spiritualism but he found the biggest comfort in the idea that he has some kind of angelic guidance. Looking back he sees all kinds of coincidences and serendipity in his life that seem to be more than mere coincidence. He now thinks that he was guided back from America to Manchester. There was a reason why he needed to be back home. He is sure that his angel was telling him something, even then.

Lee had been unhappy in the States for a long time before he left. It wasn't just the prejudice that he'd encountered. He felt a strong sense that he was in the wrong place. Nevertheless, Michael and he decided that they couldn't leave without giving it a good go. They wouldn't be able to forgive themselves if, in the future, they looked back and thought that they'd just given up. So they stuck it out for over three years, but in his heart Lee knew that America was not for him.

'I stayed for three and a half years until one Christmas Eve I asked myself if I wanted to get old in this country, and the answer was no, and I was home in three months.'

They came back to London but that too didn't feel right. Lee was older now and he wanted different things out of life. London wasn't for him and he had a strong sense of being drawn back home. He'd had some fun in the sunshine of Florida but his heart had always remained in rainy Manchester. He missed being able to call people up and be sitting in their kitchen having a cup of tea five minutes later.

'I felt I needed to have my old friends around me again. In London your friends live all over the place and you can travel for an hour to get to see everybody. In Manchester, it's a smaller community and you see people more often. Basically I wanted to get back to my roots.'

Michael and Lee travelled back up north and stayed with friends while they looked for somewhere to live. To begin with they found it very difficult to find a flat that both of them liked. They'd arranged to stay for a week while they looked around but, at the end of their trip, they hadn't found anything suitable.

They stayed an extra day, and went into an estate

agent in Didsbury who told them a flat had just become available. However, there was a catch: according to some, the flat was haunted. Lee and Michael were not deterred, however, and when they saw the apartment they absolutely loved it. They wondered why other people hadn't wanted to live there until the estate agent explained that the ghost was that of the previous owner, who'd died in the property just seven months previously.

'Within a couple of days I felt the presence of an old lady around. She seemed to be sitting in the same corner all the time. I kept seeing her in my mind's eye and at one point I said to Michael, "I think her name's Ada."'

Strange things started to happen in their flat and, although they didn't feel threatened in any way, it was disconcerting.

'The television kept going on and off. The news would be turned on at five o'clock in the morning, really loud. Funnily enough, not long after we moved in some cleaners who used to work around the outside of the building told us that the old lady used to watch the news with the volume up really loud all the time. Then the previous owner's daughter came round and we described her mother to her exactly: she was small, quite thin with broad shoulders. But most vivid to me were the white socks with slippers she wore and how she tied her hair back. And that she loved music. The daughter started laughing and said that sounded exactly like her mother, who had always said she'd come back and haunt someone. She thought it was very funny.'

Despite sharing their new flat with a noisy but harmless spirit, they were delighted to be back at home. Although Lee didn't regret his time in America he felt much more at home in Manchester. Even though he'd had the hardest times of his life there as a child, it held many of his happiest memories as well.

'I felt very comfortable as soon as I came back. It just felt right.'

And, in the end, they decided that although the ghost wasn't harming anyone, they'd prefer to have the house to themselves. They called a friend who worked as a spiritualist and he performed a kind of exorcism. After that the house seemed perfect. The nice, leafy suburb of Didsbury suited them down to the ground and they were surrounded by friends. At that time they had no inkling of why the flat's location was so perfect, but after Lee found the tumour he had good reason to be grateful that he wasn't stuck in Florida or even London, miles away from anyone he knew: the flat was literally nine minutes' walk to The Christie Hospital, one of the biggest cancer treatment centres in Europe, and Michael couldn't drive.

When he was in America and then in London Lee had constantly been troubled by the feeling that he wasn't where he should be. Now he had the reverse feeling. It was as though his new flat and this area was absolutely right. It was a great comfort during such a difficult time.

'It all seemed to fall into place. Chris Steele lived in the next street. It was strange that he should be there because he was a great help when I was unwell. It was such a relief to have a friend in the medical profession close by. When I came to reflect on it I thought that there had always been some kind of guidance in my life.'

It's almost three years now since Lee was diagnosed with cancer. He has a check-up every four months and, thankfully, it's been clear every time.

Despite the terrible experience of learning that he had cancer, and during the debilitating process of chemotherapy, Lee still felt like he was protected somehow. Everything was so much better than it could have been. He felt an overwhelming sense that his angel was watching over him.

The cliché for people who've gone through an experience such as cancer is that it changes your

life and makes you see the world in a different way.
For Lee this was only partly true. Although he saw
the hand of his Guardian Angel in the fact that he
was back among the people who loved him in
Manchester, it didn't change his faith. He'd always
believed in angels and in the spiritual world. There
was no need to reassess his life because he was
happy with the way things had worked out.

'Somebody asked me whether it had changed my
life, and I don't think it did really. It wasn't as
though I was horrible and all of a sudden I was
going to behave like an angel. I've always been the
sort of person that I am. What it did do, to a certain
extent, was make me want to achieve more, I've
stopped worrying that I don't have enough time
left, instead I believe that I've been given a second
chance.'

Lee's always loved his work and now he feels
that he has a chance to pass some of his knowledge
on. Since he first started working in a salon at the
age of just fifteen he's proved that it was much
more than just a menial job. He's risen to the top
of his profession and earned a good living out of
it and now he wants to give something back.

'To this day, not a job, but a hobby. And I enjoy
my hobby. I teach in a college now, sharing my
experience with other people. I'm about to make a

teaching DVD for young people, to hand over my knowledge to them.'

Perhaps the most important lesson he learned was that he should listen to what his spirits tell him. It always struck him as odd that he hadn't taken the voice seriously when he first heard it. He wasn't sure why he'd questioned it when he'd spent so much of his life exploring that kind of phenomenon.

'You know how it is with intuition, you question it. You get an inkling that you should be doing something but you still question whether it's something you're telling yourself or whether it's a message that you're getting from someone else, and something that you should take very seriously.'

Either way it was a message that he should have listened to straight away. The fact that he eventually paid attention probably saved his life. However, he still has the feeling that somebody is looking out for him. He feels that his life has been guided from the start and that guidance is still with him today.

'If I go looking for something it never happens, but if I stop looking and live in the moment, whatever will be will be, something always comes along. It just happens.'

Lee is also more prepared to actively ask for help now. He feels that, in difficult circumstances, he can rely on some kind of support or advice from his Guardian Angel.

'I do ask for advice more. I ask for help in certain situations and usually within three days something happens. I don't ask willy-nilly. If it's something I'm really troubled about I will ask for guidance or some kind of a sign.'

This has become more important recently as he's started to feel that it's time to move on again. He's learned to listen to whatever he's being told and, although he loves his home in Manchester, he has started to get itchy feet. It's as though the spirit that brought him back to his old neighbourhood is telling him that it has served its purpose. He was there for a reason and now it's time to move on to somewhere else. He doesn't know where yet, but he's looking forward to the challenge and is starting to prepare himself for the next stage of his life.

'I've been told to move on, definitely. It's coming but it's not time yet. I'm a great hoarder of things but I've been selling off a lot of bits and pieces. That makes me think there's going to be a move because I'm off-loading stuff so that I don't have as much to carry with me. I'm just waiting for the right time. I feel something's coming.'

The voice he heard may not have changed his life but it has made him appreciate how lucky he's been in many respects. When he became ill it was the people around him, just as much as his angelic assistance, that really made the difference and helped him pull through. The voice that he heard that night in Manchester was just the start. He firmly believes that it was his Guardian Angel, the same angel who'd been by his side throughout his life. But his Angel wouldn't have counted for so much without the help of all the people around him. For Lee the real angels are here on Earth.

'People are angels,' he says, 'or angels send people.'

RITA LYONS

Many people believe that they have a purpose in life, and that they won't die until they have fulfilled it. Some also believe that, in order to fulfill that purpose our Guardian Angels, keep us safe, ensuring that the world doesn't lose us too soon. Rita Lyons believes that, one summer's day in 1952, she was saved for a reason, and she may just be right. Here is her story.

Rita Lyons has always felt lucky to be alive. She has had a long, happy marriage and is very close to her extended family who have always supported each other. For most of her life, though, she hasn't given much thought to the day, over fifty years ago, when she was saved from near certain death. Nor did she realise, until recently, that she had been dangerously ill in childhood, to the point where it was touch and go that she would make it through. But now, when she thinks about her life and how events turned out, she believes that she has had a Guardian Angel looking after her, particularly during those times of danger, who has kept her safe and ensured that she would be able to help her family when the time came.

Her first period of danger came when she was only a little girl, and her mother would have said that her Guardian Angel was keeping her safe even then. It is only recently, after a medical check up, that Rita found out how very seriously ill she was; at the time she had no idea. All Rita remembers was that one day she felt all right, then the next she collapsed in the park and was rushed to hospital.

She didn't return home for over nine months. Rita had contracted tuberculosis, a potentially deadly lung disease, which in the 1940s was treated by keeping the patient in quarantine in a sanatorium especially set up for sufferers. Rita received the best of care and, to her family's relief, finally returned home cured.

It is perhaps not surprising that, after nearly losing her, Rita's mother and father wanted her to make the very best of her life. They encouraged her to stay on at school long after most of her peers had left to get jobs. It was a gamble for her to continue to study when she could have been working. The money she earned would have come in useful but her parents thought it was better that she invested in her future. Rita didn't always appreciate that then as much as she would later. It was difficult to be the only one of her friends without any spending money and the only one still studying in the evenings while her friends were out having fun. She would have preferred to be out at the local dances rather than stuck at home with her books. But Rita loved her parents and wanted to please them so she worked hard at school. When she passed her exams at the age of seventeen, her parents were ecstatic. Just before her eighteenth birthday, as a reward, they gave her ten pounds – a lot of money in 1952 and the equivalent of around two hundred pounds in today's money.

When her father handed her the crisp, ten-pound note and told her to buy herself something nice to wear on her birthday Rita was stunned. She'd never held that much money in her hand before. At that point she'd never worked so she'd always relied on the little bit of pocket money that her parents gave her. At first she just stared at the note in disbelief.

'It was an awful lot of money in those days. We weren't a well-off family at all. My dad had been saving up because I was finishing college so it was his way of giving me a reward for carrying on with schooling, as all my friends had been working since they were fourteen.'

When Rita turned eighteen in 1952, rationing was still underway. During the war many everyday necessities were rationed, including clothes and food, but, one by one, items were coming off the ration list and more things were available in the shops. For the first time in a long while people didn't need to feel guilty about shopping. It was becoming a leisure activity again.

This might explain Rita's state of mind that day. She was delighted but she was also distracted. She wasn't watching where she was going. She was thinking about what she would spend her money on, instead of watching the road.

It's a couple of miles from where Rita and her family lived at Newton Heath to the centre of Manchester so Rita waited at the bus stop, clutching her purse tightly in her hands. It was a warm day in late summer and there was hardly a cloud in the sky. The council had recently introduced a new bus service so once Rita was on the bus it didn't take long for her to get to the city's main shopping street.

Rita had decided to go to the big new department store in Piccadilly, located in the centre of Manchester. But to get to it Rita had to negotiate the busy road crammed with trolley buses, trams and cars. But Rita wasn't being careful. She was only seventeen and felt invincible. She barely noticed the trams and the trolley buses rattling past. She was too busy thinking about the new clothes she'd buy with the money her father had given her.

Rita didn't come into the centre of town on a Saturday afternoon very often and so she wasn't used to the cars that were now increasingly common on the streets. Petrol rationing had ended two years previously and since then the number of cars on the roads had increased exponentially.

She was just about to cross the second road towards the department store when she heard something that snapped her abruptly out of her reverie. Out of nowhere a female voice said, 'Rita! Stop!' It was so sharp and commanding in tone that she froze on the spot. If it had been a soft, gentle voice she probably wouldn't have taken any heed, but luckily the voice had enough authority that it made Rita stop dead. It shocked her back into taking notice of where she was, and to her dismay she saw that she was in the road.

Aside from the cars that were whizzing past, there was nobody near her. Nobody who could have said anything. Even if there had been anyone around, how would they have known her name? She didn't recognise the voice at all. At that same instant, almost before she had a chance to think about any of this, she heard a terrifying screech of brakes. She'd been about to step out in front of a car. If Rita hadn't stopped when the voice told her to, she would have been knocked down and almost definitely killed.

'The car was inches away from me. The driver leaned out and he looked terribly shocked. He was shouting at me, and I backed up on to the curb, terrified and upset.'

When Rita stepped back on to the curb she was physically shaking. Her good mood had vanished. From having her head in the clouds, wondering about all the things that she was going to buy, she was violently brought back down to earth. With an apologetic wave to the driver she turned round. Suddenly she didn't feel like shopping and just wanted to go back home, back to her parents. She was too stunned to think about where the voice had come from. Instead she slowly made her way back across the busy streets, checking twice every time she crossed the road, until she was back at the bus stop.

When she arrived home her mum was smiling broadly. She was expecting her daughter to rush excitedly into her bedroom to show off all the new clothes that she'd bought. Instead Rita walked in, white-faced, with tears glistening in her eyes.

Rita told her mother what had happened, thinking she would be as shocked as Rita was, but instead, her mother gave her a hug and said, 'Don't worry, Rita, it'll be your Guardian Angel.'

Rita hadn't heard about Guardian Angels before then. It was difficult to understand why an angel would take the time to save her. Rita's mother, though, didn't find the idea strange at all. She'd always been open to the idea of angels and spirits, and she regularly attended spiritual church with her sister.

Rita was still astonished by what had happened.

She couldn't explain where the voice had come from. She'd never heard anything like that before. It was too late to go out again so she just went to her room and, within a few days, she'd almost forgotten about it. Very soon she was wishing that she had just carried on to the shops. For the actual day of her birthday her father had arranged tickets for a show as well as a meal out. She still wanted to get something nice to wear. In the end she went out the day before her birthday and bought a dress, two pairs of shoes and a coat, all for ten pounds! Then her dad paid for her and some friends to go to a Chinese restaurant in Manchester and then to see a show.

It was very generous but her dad doted on his two daughters Rita and Frances, particularly after he'd come so close to losing Rita when she was a child. She didn't spend too much time thinking about her near miss after that. It just seemed like one of those inexplicable things that happen. Rita didn't hear the voice again for many years and gradually it faded from her mind.

After Rita left college she got a good job in accounting, making the time she had spent studying seem worthwhile. Not long afterwards she met her future husband, Harry, and they married when she was twenty-four. Shortly after that they had a son,

Roger. Rita wanted to give Roger the same comfortable upbringing, surrounded by family, that she had had. Life was busy and very satisfying, and she would never have had a reason to think about the voice of her Guardian Angel if it wasn't for the fact that, many years later, she would hear and see mysterious things once again.

Rita's family has always been the most important thing in her life. Happily, after she was married, she lived near her cousins and aunt and she moved into a house on the same street as her parents. Having her mother and father close by was very helpful after Roger was born. Rita continued to go in and out of her mum's house, just as she did when she used to live there.

One day, though, she had a visit from the last member of the family that she'd ever expected to see. As she passed the bottom of her stairs one day she looked up and saw a woman standing at the top. She was wearing a long, old-fashioned green dress and her red hair was plaited and wound round the top of her head like a coronet. Rita was astonished; she'd never seen this woman before in her life. As she walked past the stairs the woman said, 'Where's your mother, Rita?'

Without even thinking Rita replied, 'Oh she's next door at Auntie's.'

Later, Rita recalls, 'I couldn't believe I'd answered her, I had no idea who she was. But when I looked again she had gone. I went next door to my auntie's house, and when I told my mother that there was a lady at the top of my stairs, she just asked what she looked like. When I explained, my mother said, "Don't worry, that'll be your grandma."'

Although Rita had never met her grandmother she'd heard a lot about her. She was known as a strong, feisty woman who always stood up for what she believed in. Could the voice that Rita heard when she was seventeen have been that of her grandmother?

Rita isn't sure. 'I never heard my grandmother speak, but the sharp, commanding tone certainly fits with what I've heard about her.'

Then, not long after Roger was born, Rita heard a different voice. It was in much less dramatic circumstances but it was a comforting reminder that somebody was still watching over her.

'I was crossing the road holding on to Roger's hand. I wasn't taking too much notice of what was going on around us. Roger was trying to pull away from me, and I heard a voice saying, "Careful!"'

This time the voice wasn't as sharp or commanding. It was more of a gentle warning than the abrupt order that she'd had when she had tried to cross the road all those years before. It was as though the voice was quietly reminding her that it was still around, and that someone was looking out for her.

Later on, when her husband's father died, Rita decided to accompany her sister-in-law Jean to a spiritualist church. Although she didn't attend regularly she found it interesting and often very comforting.

'When we got there the spiritualist pointed at Jean, and said he could see an oldish gentleman laying a cross of white flowers across both of our knees. We were so surprised, because that's what we'd put on my father-in-law's coffin. A cross of white flowers.'

Thirty years after Rita had been saved, her life was turned upside down by family tragedy, and it was only then that she realised that had the angel not saved her there were people in her family who would have been overwhelmed without the love and support that she could provide.

Rita was in her late forties when her beloved sister Frances was diagnosed with terminal cancer at the age of forty-three. It was a terrible blow, especially as Rita's niece Debbie, who was just eighteen at the time, would effectively be left an orphan on her mother's death. Tragically, Rita's father was also seriously ill at the same time. So Rita and her mother found themselves shuttling between the two hospitals, trying to stay strong for both of the patients.

Her father's illness was sad but he had enjoyed a relatively long life and they could accept that it was getting near the end. Frances's illness, however, seemed particularly cruel. She still had a great deal to live for and had been looking forward to seeing her daughter grow up and eventually have children of her own.

They'd always been a close-knit family, living near to each other in north Manchester, and their only real source of comfort was the knowledge that they would stick together as they always had. Even so, it was a terrible time, particularly for Rita's mother, and for Frances's daughter Debbie.

On the day of her mother's death, Debbie was distraught, and it was Rita who was there to comfort her and sit with her. It was one of the worst days of both their lives, but Rita was glad she was able to give some comfort to her niece. But the agony was not yet over, for Rita's dad was now so dangerously ill that they felt he could not be told of his daughter's death.

It was an almost unbearable burden for somebody

who was grieving. It was hard for Rita's mother to carry on smiling for her husband while secretly knowing that their daughter had just died. But they feared that the shock of the news would kill him. As it was, just seven weeks after his daughter's death, Rita's father died as well, without ever knowing exactly just how ill Frances had been. It was a harrowing time for everyone, but particularly for Rita's mother who had been with her husband for over fifty years.

The whole family was grieving. To lose both a sister and a father in such a short space of time seemed cruel. Rita was a great source of strength to her mother and Debbie, both of whom were finding life difficult. Debbie went to live with her grandmother, and with Rita and her husband Harry living on the same street, the family were able to support each other. The grief of that time brought the family closer together.

It wasn't until Debbie got married, however, that Rita thought about how hard it would have been for her mother if she had lost Rita to that car all those years ago, only to subsequently lose her remaining daughter and husband only a few weeks apart. Her mother would have been left on her own to cope.

The death of her father and her sister, as well as

everything that happened afterwards, made Rita think back over her life. She thought back to her illness and absence from the family when she was small, and then to her miraculous escape when she was just seventeen. She had been inches away from being killed but she'd received a warning that had saved her just in time. She'd had such a full life since then and been able to help her mother and her niece at a time when nobody else could. Was it possible that she'd been saved for a reason? Her mother had always believed in Guardian Angels and it started to seem to Rita that she might have been right.

Considering how important family was to Rita's mother, it's no surprise that they wanted to hold on to their loved-ones for as long as possible. Although Rita's mother was a Catholic she'd always liked the idea of the spiritualist church because it reconnected them with their family. Even if they didn't hear a message from a loved one who had passed away, at least it was a chance to think about them for a while in a peaceful environment.

After Rita's father died her mother became even more interested in spiritualism. She'd been inseparable from her husband for almost fifty years and it was difficult to adjust to being alone. Even so, she was determined to look after herself and she never asked anybody for anything. 'After my dad died and Debbie had moved out she lived on her own. She wanted to keep her independence. If I was coming to pick her up for something, my mother told me that she often heard my dad telling her to hurry up because I'd be there in a minute.'

Could this have been her mother's imagination, or was she perhaps hearing the voice of her beloved husband, still looking after her even though he was dead?

It was always Rita's aunt who had the most interest in the spiritualist church. Her two oldest children had died when they were very young, and of course this had had a huge effect on her. Jackie had died at nine months, and Kenneth had died at the age of five. He'd been ill for several years after being paralysed following meningitis. At the spiritualist church, she received messages from them a couple of times and it was a source of great comfort to her. It is lovely to think that perhaps those two small children were watching over their mother, trying to shield her from further grief after the awful shock of their deaths.

When Rita's mother died, her aunt missed her terribly, but she was comforted by her beliefs. The two sisters had always been very close and Rita's aunt said that she was still in touch with her sister from beyond the grave. In fact, Rita's aunt told her that she visited her every day after her death, which again comforted her greatly.

Rita, too, always felt a connection with her mother that seemed deeper than the usual mother–daughter bond. It's impossible to tell whether there was something supernatural in their connection, or just the bond they had because of everything they'd been through together. In fact, Rita often knew without asking what her mother needed, and she would go round to her house without being called for. Perhaps their individual angels were talking to each other, and then whispering into their ears – who can know? But the fact remains that mother and daughter were unusually close, and the dreadful year when both her father and sister died and her niece was left orphaned merely strengthened that bond.

If Rita thought the death of her mother would put an end to any more strange experiences, then she was wrong. While on a recent holiday to Tunisia with her husband, her cousin Sheila and Sheila's husband, she again heard a voice.

'We were in a beautiful hotel with great big, wide corridors and rooms on either side. We were walking along one of the corridors when a voice said. "Hello, Rita!" A nice, soft voice, like a friend's. I turned round and there was nobody there.'

The strangest thing about that voice is that Rita's cousin Sheila heard it too, but as Sheila has a hearing aid in one ear and is completely deaf in the other, she rarely hears anything that happens around her and she needs to be touched if you want to get her attention. Sheila was astounded – she hadn't heard anything so clearly in a very long time. But she heard this voice; it was as clear as a bell.

Even though there was no obvious reason for the voice it was a reminder to Rita that there was still somebody watching over her. She found it extremely strange but also comforting. It was nice to be reminded of her mother's belief that she had a Guardian Angel.

For most of her life Rita hasn't thought too much about the voice that saved her so many years before. It is only odd moments like that in Tunisia which remind her. In her heart she knows that she could have been run over if she hadn't been stopped by the mysterious voice. She feels that she was saved for a reason. Her survival meant that she was able to help the people she loves the most.

Rita strongly believes that somebody has helped her throughout her life. She believes, just like her mother and her aunt before her, that there's a spiritual world beyond ours with another force that cares about us. She doesn't know what it is, but her experiences have convinced her that it exists.

'It just makes you realise that there is somebody there, somebody watching over us. And that's been a help and a comfort to me over the years.'

MARK HUGHES

Sometimes the signs angels send us are subtle and open to interpretation. That certainly wasn't the case for Mark Hughes, whose first angelic visitation was as visually dramatic as it was awe-inspiring. Since then, Mark has found spiritual fulfilment in following his passion, and through his music has shared his message that angels are around us, to help and guide us through difficult times.

It was a Friday morning in early autumn and Mark Hughes was just about to go to work. He had his own business that he'd built up over many years. His life was very happy, and he enjoyed a comfortable existence with his wife Amanda and his two youngest children. Contented as he was, there was nothing about his life that was out of the ordinary; he could have been any suburban businessman. But coming out of his door on that misty morning he stopped short, heart pounding, as he took in the scene in front of him.

Almost one hundred white feathers covered the canvas roof of his convertible Volvo. There were none on the ground, none on the boot, none on the bonnet – and nothing to suggest a local wag had played a prank on him; it was as if two pure white doves had had a fight above the roof of the car and flown off, leaving nothing behind them. Mark called to Amanda to come and see, and she was as shocked and puzzled as he was. Neither of them could come up with a logical explanation for the feathers and why they had landed on the roof of his car – and nowhere else.

Although at the time he was utterly perplexed, now when Mark looks back on that day, he sees the feathers as a message. At the time, despite a long-standing and deep interest in spirituality, he was unaware of the theory that white feathers are the symbol of angels. In fact, it had only been a few months before, when he'd received a leaflet advertising a song competition for World Angel Day, that Mark first heard about the idea of Guardian Angels.

Although Mark worked hard at his day job to put food on the table, his real passion was singing and songwriting. He had always been deeply thoughtful about spiritual matters, and would occasionally perform at spiritual events and festivals. Although these were small gigs, Mark soon developed a reputation for being a talented and sensitive performer.

It was the middle of 2001 when one of Mark's friends gave him the leaflet about World Angel Day, an event that was organised by the well-known angel author and broadcaster Diana Cooper. What immediately caught Mark's eye was the competition to write the official song for Angel Day.

At that point Mark had only ever played to small audiences but he'd written hundreds of songs. He wasn't particularly confident in his songwriting abilities but he enjoyed it. He always received a positive response from the people who saw him play and so he decided that he'd have a go at writing a song about angels. To his surprise, he found the music just seemed to flow. The chorus of 'The Angel Song' – 'there are angels watching over you' – was very simple and the Beatles-influenced melody was extremely catchy. As he wrote it, Mark imagined people singing along with him, and he couldn't help feeling very proud of what he'd written. So he went into a studio and recorded a demo that he then sent off to the competition.

By the beginning of October, he'd still not heard and he'd almost forgotten all about the contest. Then, just six days before World Angel Day, he received a phone call from Diana Cooper telling him his song had been chosen.

Six days was quite a deadline. He'd only played the song a couple of times and never to an audience. Mark would have to rehearse it and make sure that it was as good as it could be, but he was never one to shirk a challenge, so he said that would be fine.

During that week, Mark had a hundred copies of the CD pressed and, despite his nerves, he was as ready as he could be. It was just two days before he was due to perform when he stepped out of his house and found the roof of his car covered in pure white feathers. If he'd have known then, what he discovered a couple of days later, it may have calmed him down

On the Sunday, he and Amanda went to World Angel Day at Kensington Town Hall. By then they weren't thinking about the feathers on the roof of the car; as they drove to the event Mark was too concerned about remembering the words of the song and playing in front of so many angel enthusiasts. And when he got there he was even more nervous; he couldn't believe how many people had turned up. There were over 1,200 people in the audience.

Diana Cooper introduced the day and then she started to talk about the phenomenon of white feathers as angelic messages. Amanda and Mark looked at each other in complete shock. Because if that was true, then what had the angels been trying to tell him just two days before he received the call from Diana Cooper? Maybe they were just a friendly warning that he would have to gather his courage about him in order to perform in front of all these people! Perhaps the angels were trying to tell him that he shouldn't be afraid because they would help him, and be there with him when he sang 'The Angel Song' in front of a large audience.

Although he was shaking with nerves, Mark found the courage to get up onstage where he performed his song without incident. After the show he was thrilled when eighty-nine of his one hundred CDs were sold. Suddenly, in middle age, having only dreamed of being a working musician, he was on his way to a level of success and acclaim that he'd never imagined was possible.

Following the World Angel Day appearance, Mark subsequently recorded 'The Angel Song' with the London Community Gospel choir and he's sold thousands of copies all over the world. He's been asked to perform it many times, at home and abroad, and he's been to America several times to perform there too. World Angel Day changed his life in a way he never could have imagined. And in Mark's eyes, the feathers that miraculously and inexplicably appeared on the roof of his car that day now seem like a symbol and a foretaste of his future angel-inspired success.

Mark may never have achieved the success he did with 'The Angel Song' if it had not been for what he calls a 'hand in the back' incident that he experienced several years before.

Mark had loved music ever since he was a child.

He grew up listening to bands like the Beatles and the Eagles as well as numerous other singer-songwriters. He used to make up songs for his own amusement, occasionally playing them to his father and his girlfriends. It never crossed his mind that his songs might be popular with other people. The idea of playing in front of a large crowd terrified him. However, his attitude towards performing in front of others started to change in the early 1990s after he went away to a spiritual retreat in Dorset.

At that time, only a very few close friends and family members had heard him sing. But sitting around the campfire on the last night of the retreat, out of the blue someone broke into song. When it was over, the group sank into a slightly embarrassed silence. To this day Mark doesn't know what compelled him to stand up and sing, but he calls it his 'hand in the back' experience because it literally felt like someone pushed him in the back.

It could have been a moment of extreme embarrassment. He'd never sung in public before and he'd never performed, even in front of his family, without a guitar. His voice wavered slightly as he began his song, but he had always been able to sing well and his heartfelt lyrics sung to a simple melody were perfect for a summer's evening, with the fire dying down and the trees rustling in the wind. It was a resounding success. People really liked his performance and when they went back to bed after the campfire Mark was delighted to see everybody happy and smiling.

It was after this experience that Mark started performing in front of small groups or at churches. He was sickeningly nervous the first time he played in front of an audience, but gradually he got used to it, and finally he was hooked. It was wonderful to see so many people enjoying the songs he'd written at home in his living room. It had never occurred to him to think that they would be so popular. From then on he started taking every chance that he could to play venues around the country but he soon realised that he felt more at home playing to spiritual organisations.

His music was inseparable from his spiritual beliefs and the lyrics of his songs were often about the things that he believed in. After that first World Angel Day, there were three or four similar events in London and then he was asked to go out to LA to perform it there. By the third World Angel Day in London 'The Angel Song' had become reasonably well known, and everybody got up and sang. To hear people he'd never met sing his song was just wonderful for Mark, and he feels to this day that 'The Angel Song' has opened a door for him into a world of creative and spiritual fulfilment.

But despite his success, Mark never let it go to his head. He was still a businessman, not a professional musician. He never made a great deal of money from his music; the fulfilment he got out of it was spiritual and creative, not financial. He'd been interested in spirituality ever since he was a child, and now, through his music, he finally got a chance to express the way he sees the world to others.

Although both Mark's parents were religious – his mother was raised Catholic while his father was a Welsh Baptist – an open-minded attitude to spirituality was encouraged. This meant that while Mark didn't pick up on either of their faiths, he did become deeply interested in matters outside our realm of experience.

His parents, too, had some interest in spiritualism. In fact, after the death of Mark's grandmother, they witnessed a bizarre incident that perhaps was a pointer to Mark's future involvement with angels. It's something Mark doesn't remember as he was only four at the time. But one night shortly after his grandma died, Mark started shouting in his bedroom. His parents rushed in and Mark said that there had been a white lady in the room. What they didn't realise, until Mark's bed slowly started falling, was that it had levitated off the floor. They were utterly astounded.

Mark isn't aware of any other supernatural occurrences connected to him in his early life, but as he grew up he started exploring different belief systems. He became determined to develop his spiritual nature in order to experience the visions that he'd read about and develop his psychic abilities. It took him a long time but in the end, he says, he saw things that convinced him, 100 per cent, that the spiritual world is as real as the physical one in which we live. He is certain that there are spirits or angels out there watching over us, protecting and guiding us to live as best we can, though perhaps we don't follow their advice as we should.

Mark's own quest for spiritual development began with the discovery that he could see auras. This revelation came after attending a Spiritual Development Circle, where a group of people try to improve their understanding of spirituality. 'I can see auras fairly easily,' he explains. 'I remember being at a spiritualism centre and a woman there had such a vivid purple aura. I couldn't believe others couldn't see it. It was as if she was lit up. She was a lady who'd given her whole life to spiritual education and development and she was obviously very spiritual, genuinely so.'

On another occasion Mark saw something very strange around his then partner Barbara. Like many people who want to open themselves up to a more spiritual way of life, he'd become interested in meditation. One night, after meditating heavily for several months, he came to bed to find Barbara had a mist around her body. Mark describes it as if there was dry ice surrounding her.

'It was probably about nine inches deep and it was amazing! Eventually it faded, but afterwards I spoke to a few people and I was informed that this is what's called "the etheric web", which is a kind of spiritual energy that surrounds the human body. I think I could see it because I'd been meditating at that time, and I was in state of heightened awareness.'

But his mediation was chiefly aimed at achieving something that had fascinated him for years. He wanted to 'astral project'. Astral projection is the name for the ability to have an out-of-body experience at will. Mark had read numerous books about it and studied with experts but, for a long time, he didn't seem to be able to do it himself. For Mark, the desire to try astral travel came from the need to prove to himself what he was almost completely sure of: that the human spirit can live beyond and outside of the body and that there is another plane where spiritual beings, including angels, live. Finally, after months of sometimes frustrating practice and experimentation, Mark achieved his dream, and his meditation was so deep that his spirit left his body and travelled on the astral plane.

'To astrally travel you have to be physically asleep but mentally awake. That's what you mediate to achieve. It can take a long time but you tell each part of your body to go to sleep. So I used to start with my feet and I'd feel my feet go numb and then my legs go numb. And the last thing to happen is your hearing stops. You have to get to that stage but remain awake. So you have your eyes closed, you can't hear anything, you can't feel any part of your body but you are mentally alert and that's when you can travel. I'd almost achieved it a few times and got so excited about it that it would physically wake me up.

'So when it did happen I was trying to remain as calm as possible because I was very aware that if I became over-excited about the fact that I'd come out of my body and achieved this after so many months trying I'd be straight back in.

'Previously during meditation I'd had partial out-of-body experiences where I'd be lying mediating and I'd feel as though my arm was out to one side but I'd open my eyes and it wouldn't be. So that's an experience where your spiritual arm is out but your physical arm isn't. But with this I felt myself come out through my crown chakra [at the top of your head] and I could see my body and Barbara lying asleep.'

Having achieved it he doesn't know how long he was outside of his own body but it was long enough for him to start wondering what the next step could be.

'It's impossible to put a time on it, because time is very different physically than spiritually but I would guess I was out of my body for a few minutes. I could see the cord that connects your astral body to your physical body. I was beginning to analyse this when I was jolted back by a loud banging from outside that woke my physical body and drew my astral body back in. But the experience was amazing, absolutely amazing. After I woke up, from that moment on, I knew that you lived outside your body. That your body is not what's important.'

* * *

Despite the strength of his beliefs Mark doesn't un-critically accept everything with the label 'spiritual'. He's sceptical about spiritualism, and of many aspects of religion. As well as his two daughters with Amanda, he also has a daughter from a previous relationship, and he tries not to push his own beliefs on to them or anyone else. For Mark, his music informs people, and it's this that has been so important to him throughout his life.

The experiences he had after he first started performing totally changed the way he felt about singing and about his life in general. And he is not sure he would have been brave enough to pursue it if it hadn't been for that 'hand on the back'. Could that have been his angel giving him a gentle nudge towards the future? A future in which Mark could tell people about his experiences and beliefs? And about angels?

Like many songwriters, even those who have little or no interest in the spiritual, Mark finds songwriting a mystical experience in itself.

'I wrote "The Angel Song" in twenty minutes and it just flowed. Sometimes, when the writing is going well, you get a feeling that the inspiration is coming from somewhere, whether that's your higher self or an external source feeding it in, who knows. I wouldn't claim it was necessarily all me.'

Mark is now sixty and looking back on his life so far he says that he feels very blessed and lucky. Part of this he puts down to a belief in a Guardian Angel that's watching over him but it's not necessarily the classic image that we might have of an angel.

'I was fairly sceptical about the wings and the conventional image of the angel. People have said that they can see angels around me when I'm playing, but I'm not aware of that at all. Sometimes I feel a little like a fraud because I don't think that my belief in angels is quite the same as that of some of the people who listen to me singing about them. My theory is that angels can take any shape. They can come to you in the form of a ball of energy. Because that's what we really are, energy. But if you have a strong Christian belief, and your mental image of an angel is the archangel Gabriel, then that's what you're likely to see.

'But I do believe that we're guided and guarded and looked over. I certainly realise that I'm fortunate enough to know and to experience the presence of my Guardian Angel. I feel pretty blessed in most of my life and I'm a very contented person. I think trials and tribulations are part of life. Those big tests that you get in your life are more for your spiritual progression and well-being than anything else.'

Like many people Mark also asks the angels for help, but he says that he's not necessarily offended if they don't oblige.

'I do. I admit it! I've had some big issues and problems with my business over the last couple of years. At one point it looked like it wasn't going to survive, but I asked the angels for guidance and I just had so much help from them. But I'm very aware that life is perverse. What you think is the best thing sometimes turns out to be not at all good and sometimes what appears to be disastrous can turn out to be the best thing for you. So while I might be asking for help I'm actually saying, "Help me to discover whatever's the best thing for me." Because what I want isn't necessarily going to be what's best.'

Because of 'The Angel Song' Mark has become one of the voices of the angel movement in the UK. His song summed up many people's feelings about hidden sources of strength in the universe. This is, ironically, despite the fact that when he wrote it he knew very little about the traditions and beliefs that experts such as Diana Cooper associate with angels. The white feathers that arrived on the roof of his car that day have come to seem like not just a message from the angels but also a symbol of how lucky he has been. He has managed to balance his creative life with his professional and home life. Things may not always have been easy but, all the way through, he's had the feeling that someone, or something, has been watching over him.

ALEXIS CONSTANTINOU

It takes courage to live life on your own terms. Too often people find themselves living their life to please other people. Desperate to avoid hurting those they love, they hide their true selves. But living a lie can be destructive, and sometimes we may need a little divine intervention to help us see the truth. Which is what happened to Alexis Constantinou.

It wasn't the first time Alexis Constantinou had thought about suicide. He'd had dark thoughts on many occasions throughout his life. On one particular cold and wintry day, though, as he walked aimlessly through the grey streets of west London, he was at his lowest ebb. His depression was now so bad that he had moved away from just thinking about suicide to planning how he would go about killing himself. Death seemed like the only way out.

There were many reasons for his dark thoughts, but the worst for him was that he simply didn't like himself very much. Everywhere he went he carried a sense of shame and self-disgust. He wasn't living how he wanted to and he felt like he was living a lie. As he wandered into a small charity shop on Putney High Street in London he'd reached a decision; he was going to take an overdose.

At the time it felt as though he'd tried everything else. He'd spent hours in therapy and every therapist he'd seen agreed that he had unusual self-awareness. He knew that part of his problem was his reluctance to fully accept that he was gay. He'd been with his girlfriend Joy, for thirteen years and yet from the start he'd known that the relationship involved a denial of his real personality.

'We were both very co-dependent and hiding behind each other. Separately, we'd been through some very tough times, and as a result our relationship could be very negative at times. I think being gay and being who I really was wasn't an option for me at the time. It was so far removed from what was acceptable to me. I didn't think that I could be myself. I had to keep that part of myself hidden.'

The strain of hiding his real nature had caused him tremendous problems. It was difficult to break up with Joy because although he knew that he could never be fully committed to her as a life partner he cared about her very much and, in some ways, she understood him better than anyone. Without her he had a fear of being alone.

'I loved her and we did have a relationship in every way. But there was something missing because I was not true to myself. As the years went by it became much more co-dependent and fearful. We knew that we were stuck. I actually told her about my sexuality after the first year, yet we remained together for thirteen years.'

Joy didn't want to believe that he was really gay. Alexis says that she blocked it out and he was too frightened to break up with her. He wasn't confident that he could make it on his own. Desperately unhappy, to numb the pain he was resorting to drinking heavily, comfort eating and searching for sex with strangers.

'I was living a double life. Guilt takes its toll on you. It was alcohol, sex, compulsive behaviour. When you have an addictive personality you can use anything as a crutch to get you through life. My self-esteem was very low. What I was looking for when I had sex with strangers was external validation – for other people to make me feel I was all right.'

But external validation was the last thing that he was getting. Instead he was just increasing his feelings of guilt and worthlessness. This pattern of behaviour had been going on for at least seven years and he couldn't take it any more. And worse of all he felt that there was absolutely no one that he could turn to: his family had their own problems and they weren't able to help him; his relationship with Joy was becoming more and more difficult. And the last person he could rely on was himself – when he looked in the mirror he hated what he saw.

'I was dealing with addiction and I was in a very dark place. Despite the psychosexual counselling and addiction counselling, nothing provided the answers or help I needed. I was using food and sex to escape from the situation. I'd do anything not to deal with it, but every day I seemed to be digging a deeper and deeper hole for myself until it felt like there was no way out.'

In an attempt to lessen his guilt Alexis would tell Joy about his infidelities but that just made things worse. She was bitterly hurt and upset. Yet despite their unhappiness, their relationship continued.

Alexis can only assume that he was seeking a way out of his situation through his behaviour. But it didn't work. The infidelity that had started out as a release had become a compulsion. It had taken over his life and he was becoming more and more reckless with his own safety.

'I had a death wish. I wanted to die. I was putting myself into danger all the time. I got to the stage where I was meeting people every day, sometimes more than once a day. I'd go into situations where I wouldn't know what was going to happen. I didn't know who these people were, I didn't care – they might have been complete mad men for all I knew. At first my death wish was unconscious but as time went by it became conscious. I kept putting myself in dangerous or potentially dangerous situations in the hope that it would end. I just wanted out.'

Somehow, though, however hard he tried he couldn't seem to die. He was just piling more self-loathing on top of himself. It was a vicious circle where he was treating himself badly and encouraging the rest of the world to do the same; every time he binged on food or alcohol or sex he liked himself even less, and so the circle went on. There were only two things that made him feel better, the music he made in a band with Joy and his developing interest in spiritual healing.

His band, Colour of Spirit, had played gigs all over London and songwriting was Alexis's only real emotional outlet. But bound up with the music he was creating was his relationship with Joy; if they broke up how long would the group last? It seemed like he might be left with nothing.

To fill the spiritual void Alexis joined an organisation called the Aetherius Society and that, for a time, seemed like the answer to his problems. The Aetherius Society is an organisation founded in the 1950s by eccentric inventor George King, who said that 'space aliens held the key to the salvation both of the planet as a whole and of every individual on earth'.

George King believed that the great religious teachers, including Jesus and Buddha, were trained by what he called 'Cosmic Masters' from another planet. Although there's been some controversy and, indeed, mockery over their more eccentric beliefs, particularly that Jesus is living on Venus, members of the Aetherius Society are essentially humanitarian. They emphasise service to others, as well as the practice of yoga and meditation as the path to enlightenment. Their beliefs might sound bizarre but their emphasis on helping others had, for a time, helped Alexis to ignore his own problems. He trained as a healer and by helping other people he was able to feel better about himself. However, he was starting to feel like a fraud and a hypocrite. His attempts at healing seemed tainted. He felt guilty that he was teaching other people when he couldn't help himself. His promiscuous, uncontrolled behaviour seemed completely at odds with the society's principles. After a while it became impossible to ignore the fact that he was teaching one way of life while living another entirely.

'Eventually I left the organisation because I felt that what I was doing – my compulsive behaviour – didn't marry up with their principles – or mine for that matter. I felt like I was leading a double life. I had a genuine desire to help other people but at the same time I was running away and not acknowledging my own needs.'

At the time, Alexis had a day job as a property

manager but it didn't give him any kind of satisfaction.

'I can't remember ever being as unhappy as I was
at that point in my life. I was arguing with Joy a
lot and I was living in a property that I was
managing for my grandfather, spending my life
doing something that I didn't want to do. I felt like
I was being forced into a position of feeling responsible for somebody else's life and living somebody
else's life for them, rather than living the life that
I wanted to live. Music was my only saviour. If I
hadn't had that outlet I think I would have gone
mad.'

But on that miserable day when he walked into
the charity shop even music hadn't been enough.
He'd gone beyond the point of just putting himself
in danger. He was actively plotting his own demise.

'It was that day that I started to mentally plan
and think about what I could do,' he admits. 'I
honestly thought that that that day was going to
be the day I died.'

Going into the charity shop was Alexis's last
attempt to take his mind off his unhappiness. It
had a large book selection and he'd always liked
old books and reading about spirituality, even if he
didn't feel that he could live up to the ideals that
the books expressed.

He wasn't really concentrating, lost in his own dream world, pulling out one book and then another without noticing what they were about. Then, as he moved down the narrow aisle, he absent-mindedly tugged on a book that was tightly wedged into place. As he pulled it he made the shelves wobble very slightly and a book fell from above, landing on his head.

It bounced off, landing on the floor with the pages splayed open. He picked it up, looked at the title and had a sudden, strange epiphany. It was a book called *May The Angels Be With You* by Gary Quinn. At that point Alexis had no real interest in angels but seeing the words like that, in black and white, had a huge impact on him. He didn't believe in coincidences and he thought that the accident was sending him a clear message. It was what Glennyce Eckersley would call angelic synchronicity.

'I hadn't read much about angels before. I thought they were nice or sweet ideas but I didn't know much about them. I just thought of them as a picture in a book, not much more than some kind of fable. It sounds crazy, but when the book fell on my head, and when I saw that title, it was as if I had been sent a message and I needed to listen to what I was being told. The angels were with me. I wasn't alone. It was like a beacon of hope.'

That message saved Alexis's life. He took the book up to the counter, paid for it, and walked out of the charity shop and back down Putney High Street with a new sense of hope. However hard things might get he felt like there was somebody looking over him and giving him strength. 'I suddenly became aware that there is help and support and love. Angelic love, divine love is there. You're not alone even if you might feel as if you are.'

But the problems that Alexis had weren't going to be solved in a day. Although he walked away from the shop knowing what he had to do, making those changes was a very different matter. He was at the beginning of a long process that would lead him right back into the depths of misery, before he would make it out again.

Alexis went back home to Joy knowing, as he'd known for years, that they couldn't carry on. But still he didn't break up with her. Instead he became depressed once again. The feeling of angelic support had saved his life but he had to do the rest himself.

As somebody who'd long had strong spiritual beliefs he'd always believed that help was out there. The problem was that it was too easy to ignore it. Part of his problem was the clash between the spirituality that he aspired to and the way that he lived his life. He'd always felt that there was somebody looking over him, which, when he wanted to die, would fill him with resentment and anger. Why couldn't he just be left alone to die?

'Somehow I knew that I was protected and I could actually feel that protection. I hated it. I wanted those angelic forces that I could sense to go away and leave me alone because I wanted to die.'

Alexis didn't have the easiest childhood. His parents were wealthy, but they fought a lot. So much so that when Alexis was only thirteen he went to live with his grandparents. He stayed with first one set of grandparents in Cyprus, and then the other in London. Once again, however, he did not feel entirely happy. He adored both his grandmothers, but his grandfathers were both strict Greek Orthodox, which he found difficult.

Considering his religious background, admitting that he was gay seemed unthinkable. He struggled to accept it himself, so he had little hope that his family would understand. It wasn't until he went to music college that he found a little freedom from the strict regime of his grandfather. And it was here he met Joy, and in the beginning, although there were difficulties almost from the very start, they had a great bond. They wrote songs together and, at times, they were happy. He loved singing more than anything else and the band was the glue that bound them together. However challenging his relationship with Joy, it did at least provide him with the kind of security that he'd never had as a child.

Unfortunately he came to rely on the relationship, and by the time he was twenty-nine he and Joy had been together since they were teenagers and they could barely remember a life apart from each other. So when it finally came, their break-up was a painfully slow, drawn-out affair. When Joy finally moved out he should have been happy but he was caught in a crippling spiral of misery and regret.

Alexis admits that the year after he split up with Joy and came out as being gay was profoundly difficult for him and he became deeply depressed again. It didn't help that his parents found it very difficult to accept his homosexuality.

The hardest thing for Alexis was to accept himself. It had been drummed into him from birth that it was 'normal' to find a nice girl, get married and start a family. That he didn't want those things seemed like a defect, rather than a simple fact of nature. But as he once again plumbed the depths of despair, he had the most extraordinary experience.

'During the time I was separating from Joy I had

another really powerful angelic visitation,' he says. 'I was very unhappy and in a great deal of turmoil. I had a vision where my angel brought me to a child. The angel told me to hold the child and to love it. The child was basically me, my inner child. My understanding of the vision was that I hadn't been acknowledging and nurturing my inner child. That had damaged me. It was another affirmation to keep on learning to love myself. Which is ultimately what we all need to do.'

Alexis started to study angels. He read every book he could find and attended courses. Gradually he started to understand that angels had always been with him. He even recalled experiences from his childhood that the misery of the past few years had blotted out. There were occasions when he'd been in trouble and something that he couldn't explain had come along to help him.

'When I was very young I started to shake, and because my great grandfather had Parkinson's disease, I was terrified that I was developing it too. I was alone in Cyprus and I started to pray: "Let me not have Parkinson's, there are so many things I want to do with my life." I was shaking uncontrollably and then, from the four corners of the room, for what seemed like an hour, but it was probably only about twenty minutes, there was an intense light that came down into the centre of the room and came into my heart and pushed me backwards on to the sheet. The room was dark and it had metal shutters so there wasn't any external light. In the morning when I woke up the shaking had stopped and I felt an incredible sense of peace. From that moment I knew there was another force that we were all connected to. But strangely, it was only later, after the other experiences that I'd had, that I remembered what had happened when I was young.'

Alexis was gradually crawling out of his depression but there were many setbacks. He was still drinking too much, binge eating and putting himself in dangerous situations. His revelation in the charity shop had set him on the path to recovery but it was a slow process.

'For the first year following my separation from Joy, I was very depressed. I was still drinking and I still had my compulsive behaviours. It was a period of trying to come to terms with who I was and accepting myself. Which doesn't happen overnight.'

He continued to have counselling and his therapists confirmed what he already knew: that his problems went back to his childhood but he was still struggling to deal with them.

Almost two years after that day in the charity

shop, though, Alexis had another revelation when he met a Norwegian musician and producer called Svein Edvardsen. They shared an interest in spirituality and soon began a relationship. For the first time Alexis felt really loved and supported as the person that he truly was. Together they set up a new band called Powerlight with which they tried to promote their own philosophies of open-mindedness and acceptance. Although their relationship didn't last, the friendship that they retained afterwards helped Alexis feel that he wasn't so alone anymore. It was one more piece of the jigsaw puzzle that he'd spent his whole life putting together.

'Throughout that year after I broke up with Joy, I was starting to accept myself and live in alignment with who I really was,' says Alexis. 'I did feel very low when I wasn't with Joy, as if I was searching for somebody to be with, but what I was searching for was self-acceptance. Learning to love yourself is something that I think most people have to deal with every day.'

His relationship with Svein was a real turning point for Alexis, and from then on he began to emerge out of the darkness and into the light. Once he'd made the decision that he was going to accept the idea of angels into his life he started to experience the paranormal with almost alarming regularity.

From being interested in spirituality it now became Alexis's life's work. He had left his job in property management, which had never fulfilled him, and started working as a singing teacher. He was also becoming involved in life coaching, as well as teaching other people about angels and the spiritual world. He went back to his healing, using a system developed by the founder of the Aetherius Society, George King, whose book *You Too Can Heal* was a bestseller during the 1970s. King argued that spiritual energy is as real as electricity and that anybody can channel it for healing. While Alexis agrees with many of King's theories, angels were now at the heart of his belief system.

'It's a continual and daily revelation. Since that time I have developed my awareness and understanding of angels. I study everything I can about them and I've run groups to help other people and teach them about the subject and through that I'm learning as well. There are all kinds of synchronicities and revelations. I find white feathers almost everywhere I go and in the most unlikely places. I'm guided to certain things. There are messages that I constantly get. I've become more and more clairvoyant and clairsentient, and I actually see angels on a regular basis. Through my healing work, I've developed my abilities.'

Like many people, Alexis regards white feathers as a message from the angels. He remembers one particular incident where he feels that the angels were communicating with him directly.

'There was one occasion when I thought that I needed to have another operation on my legs because I had quite a bad circulation problem and there was a time when I couldn't walk. Svein accompanied me to the hospital and I asked the angels: if it was possible please could I not need an operation. Svein later saw a white feather and he kept it for me.'

Alexis took that as a sign that the angels were saying that he didn't need the operation. As it turned out he did get better without surgery. Not long afterwards he discovered that he could heal himself, and was able to walk.

On another occasion Alexis met an extraordinary woman at the College of Psychic Studies in London.

'I went with my friend to the Royal Marsden hospital because she was having a cancer check-up,' he recalls, 'and as it was round the corner from the College of Psychic Studies I decided to pop round there. While I was there, I met a wonderful eighty-year-old lady. And I just knew that I'd gone there to meet this woman.'

The woman described herself as a 'walk in'. It wasn't an expression that Alexis had ever heard before but she told him that it meant that her body had been occupied by a benevolent spirit.

'It was a spirit that had taken over this woman's body because she wasn't happy,' he explains. 'Sometimes what happens when a person isn't happy with their life is that another spirit takes over. The woman I met had had a major accident and it was during that time that she was taken over by that spirit.'

While talking to her Alexis kept having strange visions. He felt that there was something unusual about her but he couldn't work out what it was.

'I kept seeing a white rose while I talked to her, and before I left I said to her: "I know this sounds stupid but I keep seeing a white rose" and she said, "I'm a member of an ancient order of Egypt called the White Rose."'

Alexis also regularly sees strange patterns and shapes. 'I have seen orbs or spheres of bluish white light,' he says, 'And I have also seen beings composed of golden light which seemed kind of slatted. It's very hard to describe what this looks like – it's almost as if they're made out of a golden Venetian blind.'

Like many people Alexis also believes that the circles of white light or 'orbs' that are sometimes captured in photographs are angels.

'Orbs are considered to be angels and they seem to love music. In one of the pictures I've got I'm just surrounded by these orbs and they seem to appear whenever there's music. There are different theories as to what they are. Digital photography has been able to capture a different spectrum to regular photography and because it's a wide bandwidth they can actually capture these beings who live within many different frequencies.'

There are a large number of sites on the Internet devoted to the phenomenon of orbs. Although to sceptics they might seem like merely tricks of flash photography, or can be explained as dust or moisture on the lens, writers such as Diana Cooper regard them as Guardian Angels or other kinds of benevolent spirits. Her book *Enlightenment Through Orbs* examines orb pictures and interprets what the orbs mean in each circumstance. However, some people, including Alexis, believe that they don't merely experience orbs in photographs, but in reality as well.

'Since being interested in orbs I've actually been able to experience them clairvoyantly,' he says. 'I can now sometimes feel or see energies and spirits.

It can be a little bit scary at times but I'm used to it and people just think that I'm crazy and that's fine!'

Alexis has experienced many different types of visions and spirits. Once, when he was making a film about positive thinking to put on YouTube he had a vision of faces.

'A huge face appeared to me,' he says. 'It was exactly like one of the stone faces that you find on Easter Island. It was very strange.'

Nine different faces appeared to him and the experience made him feel highly emotional. Even more extraordinarily, after seeing the faces appear, Alexis saw something that seemed to be straight out of a children's story. When the faces had faded, he saw an angel. 'Usually you think of angels as huge but this one was very small. It looked more like a fairy, like one of those Victorian paintings of cherubs with wings. Almost like a child but not human necessarily. It appeared in human was white and it was winged. It was about three feet tall and it radiated a deep sense of peace.'

For Alexis, though, the concept of 'angels' is about more than just mystical winged figures. He senses angels in all kinds of different phenomenon.

'It might be an energy that you feel,' he says. 'It might be a colour, it might be a breeze. Or you might have a sense of a sound, or music, a light, a knowing. I think that angels can appear physically if they need to. If you read accounts of angels there are situations where they can appear as normal people.' As in Lalla Dutt's story.

As he's become increasingly fascinated by the idea of angels, Alexis has also started to research other areas of the paranormal and the spiritual. He notices what he considers to be signs and guidance everywhere. He's a firm believer in what's known as the '11:11 phenomenon'. This is the belief that seeing the number '11 11' more than you'd expect by pure chance is a sign of angelic presence.

'I saw it so regularly, that I researched the phenomenon and discovered that it's an angelic gateway, because the numbers 11 11 placed next to each other look like an actual gateway. So it's a time when there's a doorway between the angelic world and this world, and you can access greater inspiration through them. What it means when you see "11 11" is that the angels are giving you a message that they're there.'

Alexis says that he keeps seeing the same number when he looks at a clock, or in numerous other situations.

'It's not just on a digital clock. It could be the time on a microwave or an oven, or I might pass a doorway and look and it would be "11" on both sides of the doorway. It could be on a gate, it could be two buses passing each other and they're both 11. Time and time again I see this on registrations and number plates. I've seen it too many times for it just to be a coincidence. I don't believe in coincidence. I don't think that word should be in the dictionary!'

For Alexis angels are now as natural a part of his life as eating or breathing. Although he still has moments of depression, the strength he receives from his beliefs means that he has never gone back to feeling quite as low as he did that day he walked into the charity shop.

'Even the other day I felt extremely lonely and in the dark moment of loneliness I felt that presence again,' he says. 'I think that love and support is there, not just for me but for everybody. But I think my understanding has brought me to feel and know when that guidance is there.'

Where once Alexis desperately waited for help he now says that he asks for it whenever he can. He believes that the angels will respond to his needs, as long as he asks them.

'They only intervene when they have to,' he says. 'I'm now more aware of that. I think it's only because I was about to take my own life that they intervened last time. Otherwise you have to ask for their help.'

Even more important for Alexis is that he feels comfortable now in offering help to other people. Where in the past he felt ashamed of claiming to be a healer because of the problems in his own life, he's now started his faith healing again. He says that he has had some very successful results.

'I'm constantly developing as a healer and learning new ways to supplement the healing. It's a mixture of positive thinking and channelling energy and of course I ask the angels to help me or to help the people. For instance I tried to help a lady in her eighties who'd had quite a bad accident and was due to have an operation. I was thrilled when a little while after the session she called me to say she didn't know what I'd done to her, but the doctors didn't think she needed to have the operation any more.'

As well as learning more about the world of angels Alexis has also become passionate about telling other people about them. He has recorded his own programme about positive thinking for YouTube and he dreams of teaching other people even as he learns more himself.

'The YouTube programme came out of a trip to America and learning about something called the

"Inner Life" and I became an Inner Life workshop leader.'

As well as this he's still studying and reading. One of the most inspirational books he's read was, unsurprisingly, the one that fell on his head that day. *May The Angels Be With You* is a book that teaches people to connect with their own Guardian Angels. According to the author, Gary Quinn, if you want something then all you have to do is ask for it.

Alexis loves sharing his own beliefs with people now, however strange they might appear to other people. Having had to deny his true nature for such a long time it's important for him to be honest about how he feels. In many ways what he believes now is no more extraordinary than what he was taught as a child. And, although Alexis's strict Christian upbringing might have made his life difficult as he struggled to come to terms with being gay, he still has a lot of reverence for aspects of Christian belief and faith in general.

'I'm doing a course right now called "The Sacred Magic Of The Angels". It's a twelve-week course where I'm learning the origins of Christianity, Islam and Judaism. It's going right back into pre-Biblical times, way back into Ancient Egypt.'

Although sceptics might think that Alexis's beliefs

221

are unrealistic, naive or impractical, the reverse is true. For him believing in angels is rooted in pragmatism. An angel saved his life; they help him on a day-to-day basis. Whether it's actually 'true' in a scientific sense doesn't matter to him.

'You could argue that what happened was a pure psychological coincidence – that I created it with my own mind,' says Alexis. 'A sceptic would view it like that. Whether that's true or not is not the issue. It did change my life and I didn't kill myself. That's what matters. My understanding now, through my study of angels, is that they are part of us anyway. They're archetypal energies. Everything is within you. You could argue that it is of your own creation because everything is. We're part of God. We're all part of God. For want of a better word.'

As well as its deeper, spiritual resonance Alexis's belief in angels is like a tool. He believes, like Gary Quinn, that if he asks for something and he really needs it he will get it. One example is his recent desire to attend the course of positive-thinking guru Louise Hay in America. Louise Hay is the author of *You Can Heal Your Life*, one of the most successful positive-thinking books of all time. She's best known for her belief that disease and illness are caused by negative thoughts and that they can, conversely, be cured by positive thoughts. Although some of her views are highly controversial, such as her belief that serious congenital illnesses such as cystic fibrosis are caused by negative thinking, *You Can Heal Your Life* has sold over 35 million copies to date. She is one of Alexis's biggest inspirations. Unfortunately she charges enormous sums for her courses and there was no way that Alexis could afford it. However, he applied her methods of positive thinking. He told himself that he would go to America. Somehow, more work arrived and he managed to find the money.

'Out of "no way" there's always been a way,' he says. 'When I was going through the year of hell after breaking up with Joy, I studied Louise Hay's work, which was all about positive thinking and I later went to the States to learn how to teach her work. There was no way I could afford to pay for this course because it cost three or four thousand pounds but I did a lot of affirmation work, where you repeat positive statements. Things conspired to help me to go and I went. Suddenly I'd have work or clients or whatever and that would make it okay. When you don't have fear, when you change your fear into trust, your path becomes smoother. When you ask for help you get it.'

Equally Alexis believes that he managed to find the dream home that he's currently living in with the help of the angels. When he and Svein were first planning to live together they weren't impressed by the majority of the houses that saw within their price range. On their way to see yet another unsuitable looking house, they stopped in to see a house that was far too expensive. Instantly they fell in love with the house, but it seemed impossible. 'Everything went against me living here, but I kept believing and I kept asking to live here and I did. Then later on I ran angel groups and workshops here in this space because there's a very special energy here. It has a lot of trees. I feel really protected in this place. It's almost like this house wants me to be here.'

But it's not always as simple as that. There are some things that Alexis has asked for that he hasn't received. He thinks, in retrospect, that it's just as well.

'If things aren't meant to happen then you won't get them,' he says. 'An example is that I recently applied to the *X Factor*. I got through the first three rounds and I found out today that I'm not through to the main show. I was kind of hoping in a way that I wouldn't get through because it would've meant I wouldn't be able to keep working with Svein; I'd have been contracted to them for a year and a half if I'd made it. Even if you really want something to happen, if it's not right for you then you won't get it.'

Equally, not all the spirits that Alexis has seen are quite as benevolent as the angels. When he first moved into his dream home he noticed many strange goings on.

'I kept meeting neighbours and they'd tell me the house was haunted. Even the man at the gym knew it was haunted.'

To begin with Alexis just had a sense of something out of the ordinary and a feeling that they weren't alone.

'I had a very distinct sense of being watched when I first moved in. It was like a dark shadow. There's a swing outside and apparently it used to go round and round by itself but they took off the swing and just the frame is there now. I have quite a few friends who are psychics and one of them told me that the groundskeeper had a son who was mentally handicapped and he died in an accident by the swing. His spirit was trapped and he hadn't moved on completely. I think one of the reasons I came here was to help him move on.'

Alexis performed a special ritual to exorcise the spirit and he says that he hasn't experienced anything sinister since.

Seeing the world through a spiritual prism has

made an enormous difference to Alexis's life. He might suffer the same disappointment and hurt as he did before but the feeling that there is more to the world than meets the eye makes it easier for him to cope. Sceptics might not believe that everything he has seen is real but, for Alexis, that is missing the point. He believes that life is about creativity and that spirituality, at least in part, is about choosing to see the world how you want it to be.

'Imagination is very linked to psychic ability. It is the faculty we have that allows us to connect with the unseen realms. Ultimately my understanding now is that we are the creators of our own reality and whatever we believe does become the truth for us. So rather than something that's going to keep us in a state of fear, why not believe the most positive and beautiful thing? You've always got a choice.'

This doesn't mean that Alexis believes he's simply made up his experience of angels in order to make himself feel better. It means that he's chosen to see the world in a different way and become receptive to the energies that surround each of us. It's as much about positive thinking and choosing love as it is about spiritual beliefs. He believes that there's something guiding everybody but he's open to the idea that the angels are within us.

'We're always being guided. Everyone is. But I think that sometimes we don't listen. Things block us, whether it's our own behaviour or our own negative thinking. We might have intuition or impulses to do certain things but we don't listen. It's a process of learning how to trust yourself. You just have to remember to be in the energy of love rather than in the energy of fear. We've always got a choice. Do we choose love or do we choose fear? It's a constant reminder to myself to come back to that energy. If I'm fearful or if things aren't going my way it's about being still and being in your centre and connecting with yourself and the angels. It's something I do on a daily basis. There's a spark of God in all of us and we're all one being.'

For Alexis the main revelation that he received the day he walked into the charity shop was that he could decide how to see the world. He didn't have to accept the view that his way of life was wrong or immoral. He didn't have to feel that the dark experiences in his life had somehow scarred him for ever.

'I now see everything that happened in my life as a major blessing. I now look at negative experiences as great teachers that help us to develop. Whenever we go through something that seems

227

negative it's not negative at all, it's just a transitional period. It's taking you to where you need to be.'

The day in the charity shop was the beginning of a new acceptace of life for Alexis. His way of looking at the world, refusing to accept the idea of coincidences, means that he sees new miracles almost every day. His appearance on *Angels* delivered another moment of angelic synchronicity as he met Glennyce Eckersley, who has co-authored a book with Gary Quinn. Then, as he went through the doors into the studio, a white feather fell right past him.

JUSTINE EMERY

There are times in everybody's life when they need to find some extra strength and keep faith with what they believe. Who knows where that strength comes from, but in Justine Emery's case, she's pretty sure that an angel helped her stay steadfast in the face of overwhelming medical evidence.

By the time she was twenty-nine, Justine Emery had a life that was the envy of others. She had been married for three years to Richard, a man she adored, and she had a good job working for a recruitment consultancy, which paid well. However, although she enjoyed her job, it was not what she wanted to do with her life. The job that Justine had wanted all her life was one that so many women take for granted: she wanted to be a mother.

But, despite trying for many years, Justine and her husband had failed to conceive, and finally Justine sought medical advice. But she wasn't prepared for what her doctor had to tell her, and the news was devastating.

Two years beforehand, at the age of twenty-seven, Justine's appendix had burst, leaving her with peritonitis, an infection of the lining of the abdomen. Although the doctors had operated, they hadn't managed to remove all the infection, it had caused adhesions in her ovaries. Adhesions are a complication of infection where two tissues that ordinarily would be separate are joined together. Tubal scarring and adhesions are a common form of infertility.

'I went to my GP after Richard and I had been trying to get pregnant for a while. He referred me to the Queen Charlotte Hospital in Hammersmith. They discovered that one of my tubes had been very badly damaged through infection and there were a lot of adhesions.'

So it was that, at the age of twenty-nine, Justine sat in a nondescript office of the Queen Charlotte Hospital in London where a doctor broke the news to her that she had to have a hysterectomy. And in the blink of an eye, Justine's world fell apart.

She'd been with Richard since she was just twenty-one, they got married when she was twenty-six and they'd always assumed that one day they would start a family together. She knew that she had some health problems but to hear the news told so bluntly was a cruel blow.

"I was absolutely devastated. At twenty-nine, when you've been trying for a child for four years, it's so hard to take. Being a mum was all I wanted to do.'

Many people in the same position would go through a stage of denial first, then grief, and then finally acceptance. But Justine had a strong sense that she was *meant* to be a mother and she would not give up on this dream. Despite the risks, and against medical advice, she wouldn't give her consent for the hysterectomy. The doctors tried to persuade her that her health depended on it but she wouldn't budge.

From a very early age, Justine had been aware of presences around her, and although she was yet to meet her Guardian Angel, she had the unshakeable belief that something was warning her not to go down the path of a full hysterectomy. Justine was a young woman, but the strength she gathered from this unknown presence helped her to stand firm before her doctors who had many years of medical experience behind them.

'I just knew that it wasn't the right thing to do. The doctors said that if I had fallen pregnant over the past two years, which would have been a miracle in itself, the baby would not have survived because of the poison that had been seeping into my womb. I knew I needed an operation to get healthy again, so I told them to do whatever they had to do, to chop out whatever they had to chop out, but I insisted that they must leave me my womb and at least one set of ovaries. I would not consent to the operation otherwise.'

The doctors weren't sure what to make of Justine's determination. They wanted what was best for her and were concerned that her desire to have a child meant that she was taking a massive risk with her health and well-being.

But Justine was not intimidated or cowed by the doctors' experience and knowledge. She'd had plenty of experience with hospitals when her mum had suffered a serious illness when Justine was young, and she was confident that she knew what was best for her own body.

'The doctors were taken aback by my stubbornness. I don't think surgeons are used to being questioned. In my opinion, people sometimes mistakenly think that medical word is law. But when my mum was sick there were occasions when I thought that things weren't as they should have been. So I decided I should go with what I felt and not what the doctors told me needed to be done.'

Without her consent the doctors would never perform an operation as serious as a hysterectomy but, even so, there was a nagging worry in Justine's mind. She had a terrible fear of coming round after the operation and finding that, after all, they had decided that a hysterectomy was the only option.

Justine was admitted to the hospital the day before her operation, and that night, she tried desperately to make sure they understood what she wanted.

'I was very upset because I wanted to make sure

that they were clear on that. I didn't want to wake up and find that everything was gone.'

Once she was left alone, she found sleep impossible to come by. The ward was noisy, but it was the thoughts and fears that were running through her mind that kept her awake. What would the surgeons find when they operated on her? Could the infection be worse than they had initially thought? Would they decide to perform a full hysterectomy on her after all, against her instructions? It seemed to her that the surgeons were offering her very little hope at all, and during that long dark night, her dream of having her own baby seemed to be slipping away.

As she lay there, staring at the ceiling and fretting, Justine became aware of a strange presence. She had a feeling that she wasn't alone. When she looked at the end of the bed she saw something astonishing. It was a white figure, a woman, veiled in light, sitting there and transmitting an extraordinary feeling of peace.

'I've been lucky enough to get a better look since so now I know what she looks like. But then I just saw a shape of light. I could tell that she was a woman but she was more like a white light. I couldn't look and see through her, she was solid. It looked like a substance but it wasn't, it was an energy. I couldn't work out why she was the shape she was. I later realised that she was wearing a nun's outfit but I couldn't see that at the time. I could just see the outline of this lady. She sat on the end of the bed and she stayed with me the whole night. She was a very calming influence and I knew that everything was going to be all right.'

This wasn't the first time that Justine had experienced the paranormal. As a child growing up in the quiet, suburban environment of Sudbury in north London she'd often seen, heard and felt things that nobody could explain.

'Once I was on holiday, I think I was about eight or nine, and I remember seeing a girl in the room we were in. She was in swimwear and she had wet hair. There was nothing threatening about her at all and it later transpired that there was a little girl who'd stayed in that room who had drowned. And once at a service at a spiritual church, there was a psychic giving a message and I could actually see the person's spirit hovering over him. Things like that have happened.'

She's happy to call those past experiences 'ghosts', for want of a better word. She believes that there are spirits of all different kinds all around us. But she felt sure that the visitor the night of her operation was something very different. It was her Guardian Angel. In fact, she'd first had the sensation of a Guardian Angel looking out for her when she became ill with appendicitis.

'I got dropped off from college because I wasn't feeling very well. And that's when my appendix burst. There was nobody due back at the flat but my flatmate came home unexpectedly early and called an ambulance for me. I remember that energy then, feeling aware that something was protecting me, and was responsible for sending someone back home to help me.'

Often Justine's spiritual or supernatural experiences took the form of dreams or visions. She doesn't claim to be psychic but she has had experiences that she feels were warnings or predictions of what would happen in the future. Even when she was a child there were moments when she had

On one tragic occasion, when Justine was in her teens, she dreamt that she was trying to catch the hand of her then boyfriend's twin brother before he fell over the edge of a cliff. But he kept slipping through her hands. It left her feeling very uneasy. She knew something was going to happen, but she didn't know what.

Three weeks later Justine was at her boyfriend's house. It was the morning of New Year's Eve and they were happily discussing how they were going to see the year in. Justine's boyfriend's brother hadn't got out of bed yet but they didn't think anything of it until they heard a commotion and their happiness was shattered.

'His dad came flying down the stairs and said: "He's dead." He was only twenty years old; it was tragic.'

Justine was still administering CPR when the ambulance arrived but he was already gone. His death remains a complete mystery to this day.

But the presence on the end of her bed that day in Queen Charlotte's Hospital was very different to anything that Justine had experienced before. The energy that she felt radiating from it may have been very familiar but she'd never seen anything like it before, never before did it seem to have a shape, and a personality. This wasn't simply energy, this was something that managed to be incredibly powerful yet indescribably comforting at the same time. Even more amazingly, she felt that this light in the shape of a woman was communicating with her.

'I didn't see her speaking. It was more like thoughts and feelings were dropped into my head. Thoughts that said: "Everything's going to be fine. You need to be calm. You're fine. You're safe."'

Most of the time, she sat at the bottom of the

bed, but when Justine started to feel more upset, she'd move closer, and holding her hand – and then, although Justine wouldn't see her move, she'd be back at the bottom of the bed.

'Her presence was very comforting, very calming. When I went down into theatre, even though I couldn't see her, I still had the feeling that she with me.'

When Justine woke up from her surgery, the doctors had good news. Although she wasn't in perfect shape things weren't as bad as they'd thought.

The surgeons told her that they'd been able to free up one tube. They couldn't clear everything, but they couldn't believe how healthy the womb was, despite all the adhesions.

It was a great relief but in some ways the desperate hope was more emotionally draining than having the door slammed in her face; with bad news you know that you've just got to get on with it, but with a little hope comes the knowledge that you need to keep fighting. And although Justine felt vindicated in her refusal to have the hysterectomy, she was still only a little closer to her dream of having a child. It would still take a miracle for her to become pregnant naturally.

However, there were other options. As soon as

she left the hospital she began researching the possibility of IVF treatment. It seemed like her only hope.

'You need eight viable eggs for IVF and I had twenty-two. They did a good job for me, they really did.'

When she heard back from her NHS Trust about IVF, though, her hopes were dashed. Despite being in perfect health – Justine didn't smoke or drink and was the right weight for her height – she was turned down.

It was a cruel blow. Justine had assumed that IVF was designed for people like her. What made it worse was that it seemed so arbitrary, almost like a lottery. Her local NHS trust turned her down when perhaps another would have given her a chance. Despite having a serene and optimistic nature, for the first time Justine felt hurt and upset.

'I was very angry and frustrated because I'm quite optimistic and I like to find solutions to problems. It just seemed to me that I'd overcome one obstacle just for another to be put in my way. I never stopped hoping, never stopped wanting a baby of my own but sometimes it just seemed too hard.'

Once the anger had subsided, though, she remembered the energy of the night before her operation that told her everything was going to be all right and once again she had the overwhelming belief that she would, one day, have a child.

Before her visitation from the shining white light, Justine used to feel as if everyone in the world except her and Richard were able to have children. 'I didn't want to be jealous or bitter, but I found it hard. All I could think, was "Why can't *I* have a child." But after that presence sat on my hospital bed and held my hand I felt different. I felt stronger.'

The catalyst for her new feeling of strength and confidence was a strange vision she had while she was sitting quietly one day. She dreamt that she was taken into a room. There were lots of little energies in this room, similar to the white light she had seen in hospital, but smaller. She was told that each energy was a child that was yet to be born, and that she should choose one.

Each 'energy' didn't seem to have a physical form yet but she could somehow sense the physical form that they would one day take.

'Someone was standing beside me and they said: "Pick one" and I said: "I can't pick one over the other." Then one just came into my arms and I looked down and it was a little girl. I was given her name, Trinity. Someone said. "You're going to have a baby, we've just got to get the baby to you. But the babies are here waiting for you.'"

If it was impossible for her to have children naturally and the NHS would not provide IVF treatment then Justine knew she had to find another way. She was more sure than ever that she would have a child but she still wasn't sure how.

'I just knew it was going to be okay. And then I started noticing a certain advert in the magazines at work. Every time I'd see a magazine like *OK!* or *Hello!*, it would be open on that page. It sounds very bizarre! Then my friend phoned me and said: "Have you seen this advert in the magazine?"'

The advert was for an open day at an assisted conception clinic. The ad gave little information, just the date and a phone number to call to book a place. Justine attended the clinic but although she couldn't afford the treatment, she got accepted as an egg donor. She donated eggs for two women, and that paid for her IVF.

It was what she'd been waiting for. But even so, medical science didn't offer her much hope of success. Originally doctors had told her that there was only a 5 per cent chance that IVF would be successful for her. To Justine, though, it didn't seem like a shot in the dark. She had absolute certainty that she would soon be holding the child that she'd seen in her vision.

'It wasn't a case of blind faith, where you want something so much you think it's going to work,' she insists. 'I knew that this was already in place; I just had to go through the motions. Although there was that "want" to be a mum it was a different emotion to the way I had been feeling before my vision. It was peaceful. There wasn't that ache that you have when you want to have a child. I had a feeling of knowing that she was there, waiting to come to me, and it was going to be okay.'

Not long after her treatment started Justine discovered that she was pregnant. It was a moment of pure joy but it didn't come as a surprise to her. She had never doubted for a second that the treatment would be successful.

However, her story was not over yet. When the day of the birth arrived she would once again find not just herself, but also her baby, in mortal danger. Once again she would need the assistance of her Guardian Angel.

It was to be one of the best days of Justine's life – she was finally going to meet her daughter for the first time – but it didn't start that way. Early on the doctors knew that there were complications. As her contractions got closer there was a rising sense of anxiety in the delivery room but they were still telling her that everything was okay. People were coming in and out, the midwife was joined regularly by doctors and the baby didn't seem to want to be born. Justine became concerned that they weren't doing the right thing. The doctors and nurses told her that she should just relax but she wasn't convinced.

'They weren't listening to me and I was looking at the printout that they'd left on the bed, because things were going pear-shaped, and I could see the heartbeat wasn't recovering.'

As the doctors debated what to do she could only wait in terror. It seemed so cruel that things should go wrong now, after she'd been promised that everything was going to be okay.

'It was awful. It had taken me eight years from starting to try for a baby to the point where I was almost able to hold her in my arms. And now I had this horrible cold feeling of dread. I thought: "No, not now, it can't go wrong now."'

The hospital decided that they needed to operate but it was too late.

'My daughter had gone back-to-back and got stuck in my pelvis. They wanted to do an emergency C-section but they didn't have time. I'd lost quite a lot of blood and things weren't looking good.'

That's when she saw her Guardian Angel again. As before she was sitting at the end of the bed, but this time Justine saw her much more clearly. This was when she realised that her guardian was a nun.

'She has dark eyes and dark hair. She's very slender, very, very slim. And from the habit that she had on, I don't think she is English. It was a dark, navy colour rather than jet black. I can't explain it but I got the feeling that she was French. She isn't very old, I think in her late twenties.'

As before the angel transmitted a feeling of immense calm and serenity. All at once Justine knew exactly what she had to do. It wasn't going to be easy but she had a new source of strength and determination.

'The room was full of people and everybody seemed to be panicking but now my angel was with me again I felt really calm. It was as if I could feel what I had to do and it didn't matter what they were saying. It wasn't an instinct, it was as if someone was telling me that the doctors were wrong. So when the doctor said, "She's turned round, it's fine." I knew he wasn't right.' So I did what I had to do to get it done. Which was to push as hard as I could; it was very painful and I had lots of stitches afterwards!'

At last the baby appeared but she didn't make a sound. It wasn't clear whether she was breathing. She was taken away immediately for tests.

'It was fine,' says Justine. 'I was so calm. When she came out she wasn't crying and they took her away and everyone was holding their breath but I knew it was going to be fine. When they brought her back to me, they were smiling and I knew that I was right not to worry. The midwife put her in my arms, my baby girl looked into my eyes and that was that.'

The dream that she'd had for so long had at last come true. Justine was now the mother of a beautiful, healthy baby girl and she could not have been happier. The only thing that surprised her was that the baby in her arms didn't look like the child that she'd been given in her vision. That child had been blonde and blue-eyed. This one was much darker, with dark hair. But that didn't matter. And, as the dream she'd had before the IVF suggested, she called her 'Trinity'.

'The name Trinity is quite unusual for a girl but it was given as a sign, an acknowledgement of a gift from above. And because she was given to me by angels her middle name is "Angel". And because my grandmother is very much spiritually present in my life and her name was "Rose", so she's Trinity Angel Rose.'

From the start Trinity Angel Rose was the apple of Justine's eye and even now she can't help gushing with pride when she talks about her daughter, now five years old.

'I know everyone thinks their kids are lovely but if you could see Trinity, she is just the most beautiful, wonderful, lovely child,' Justine smiles whenever she talks about her daughter. 'She has her moments like anyone but you couldn't ask for a nicer child. She fits her name really well. She's an absolute poppet, she really is.'

Justine's relationship with Trinity is all the more poignant because she had a very troubled childhood herself, particularly in her teens. Inevitably, although she's long since come to terms with this, the birth of her own daughter brought some of those memories back. It made it all the more important to give Trinity a better childhood than she'd had.

'I had a very difficult childhood and then my mum was very sick and it all culminated in my late teens when I was put in care,' she says.

At that time she felt like there were very few

people that she could turn to. Although she was taken away from her family for her own good it was a very frightening experience for a teenager. Looking back now she says that she felt very much alone.

'I felt very unhappy. That's not my natural demeanour. I'm a very bubbly, outgoing person but with all the issues that were surrounding home I became very isolated and very lonely.'

Although her background wasn't religious she found comfort in the Christian stories that she'd read.

'I was quite into reading the children's Bibles and things like that, even though my parents are not religious at all. I used to find it very peaceful sitting in a church. When my mum was sick I found it a very peaceful, calming place to be but you don't realise what you're doing when you're a child like that.'

It was in her teens, at her lowest point, that she first had the sense of a spiritual force giving her support and comfort. It was the same energy that, much later on in hospital, she would associate with the mysterious nun. As well as her spiritual awakening, though, Justine also believes that the difficult times she went through as a child and in her teens helped give her the strength that she would need later to fight for the child she felt she was destined to have. They also gave her a very compassionate attitude towards people trapped in their own difficult families.

'I learned a lot about myself from it,' she says. 'It made me more forgiving. It helped me to understand people better and brought a new sense of compassion.'

One difficult part of Justine's childhood was having to spend so much time in hospitals during her mother's illness. It could have made her fearful of them later on but instead she says that it toughened her up. It was an environment that she was, sadly, very used to and she was aware that many of the medical staff were wonderful people doing an incredible job.

Justine is determined to provide Trinity with a happier childhood than she had but at the same time she doesn't want her to feel like she has to somehow make up for what happened to her.

'I do want to give her a better life than I had but I don't want to put any expectations on her. She's her own person and you've got to put your own thoughts, feelings and fears away and let them discover things themselves. You have to let them learn and make their own mistakes.'

For Justine everything that happened in her life has helped make her the person she is today.

'If you hold on to negativity and bring it with you it doesn't do any good. And that's the spiritual side that I've found. The ability to cut off the negative. Good things can come out of bad situations, if you can learn from them. And in the end, it makes you a better person.'

The fact that she's so happy with the way her life turned out makes it much easier for Justine to accept and come to terms with her difficult teenage years. It doesn't mean that she's downplaying the effects of an unhappy childhood but it does mean that she's been able to put it behind her.

Justine is also very aware that if she hadn't had such strength of character, and the support of her Guardian Angel then Trinity would never have been born. Her decision to trust her instincts on the day she went into hospital may seem easy in retrospect but the odds were stacked against her. It would have been much easier to have accepted what the medical professionals said. Instead she decided to fight.

'I'm quite laidback but I am a wasp in a bottle for getting things done. Mentally I am very strong. I don't think that I'm normally stubborn but in this instance, I was, definitely. Because I knew that I had to follow what I was being told instinctively and, if you like, otherworldly. Because that was right and what they were doing was wrong. And it proved itself. Because I had my daughter and she is, touch wood, fine and healthy. If I'd listened to them and had the hysterectomy she wouldn't be here.'

It's hard to say how far Justine's own strength of character comes from her belief in her Guardian Angel. The feeling that she has somebody watching over her has helped give her a confidence and feeling of security that many people lack. It meant she was able to fight for her beliefs because she had such certainty that they are true.

It's still a mystery, though, why her angel takes the form she does. Justine thinks that one day she may find the answer but, for now, she's just happy that she has somebody watching over her.

'I thought of her as my white lady, when she first came, and now I think of her as my Guardian Angel. I know she's an angel but I've never been given a name for her. If at some point I know more, then great but until then I'm happy with what I've got. It's just nice to know that there's someone up there keeping an eye on you.'

It is intriguing, though that the angel appears to her in the form of what appears to be a French nun. She says she has no connections with France or the Catholic faith whatsoever.

Nuns have been staples of ghost stories for generations. However, for Justine, the distinctive thing about her nun is not so much her appearance but the strange, calming energy she gives off. That sense of well-being that she experienced, even before seeing anything, has convinced her that her strange visitor is more than just an apparition.

'I see her as an angel, not as a ghost. I think there are probably spirits of all different types around but she definitely, to me, has an angelic feel. She didn't move in a way you'd imagine a ghost – whooshing along! Instead, it was her energy that was so distinctive. I've seen other kinds of spirits, and this was different to anything I've seen or felt before. I would say she was definitely an angel.'

Her concept of what an angel is comes from her very individual religious beliefs. She doesn't believe in organised religion in a strict, conformist sense but she does believe that there are certain truths within all of them.

'I've done a lot of research into different faiths and there are similarities in each of them. But the one common denominator each faith has is this belief in messengers or bringers of good. They're the angels. They're the only consistent thing there is. Right across the board, through the ages, there have always been these messengers or angels or whatever you want to call them. For me they're a core part of the set-up. I think angels are very different to other spirit energies that you might get.'

Justine's belief in her Guardian Angel, and in the spiritual world generally, has had a dramatic effect on the way she sees the world. It has made her less materialistic and better able to appreciate the more important things in her life. She was once highly paid and 'successful' in material terms but she says that she feels much happier now with her spiritual rather than material wealth.

'I had a successful job, apparently! I got a great pay cheque but I worked long hours and my quality of life suffered. I'm far happier being poor and being at home. I'm always skint but I'm a very lucky lady – I'm rich in other ways!'

For Justine, her faith is more important than any of the trappings of success; it's where she has found her strength in difficult times, and it's made her the person she is today.

'If you have faith there are a couple of really lovely things that go with it,' she says. 'Faith is undoubtedly a great source of strength when you're going through difficulties, because you don't ever feel alone and isolated. I have been in that lonely place in the past and it's a horrible way to feel. But faith has also made me more open-minded and less judgemental and I look at things in a different way. I look at troubles as lessons and problems as learning. I feel very lucky to have faith, and to have been visited by my Guardian Angel. But I don't think there's anything wrong with people who don't believe, and I don't feel like I have to convert them. I just think it's a shame because by closing their minds to the possibility of angels and spirits, they're missing out on being sensitive to the mysteries of the universe.'

Justine also rejects the idea that the vision of a nun was a product of her own mind at a time of great stress and emotion.

'I've been aware of a spiritual presence at very positive times in my life too. I'm quite comfortable with the idea of a Guardian Angel because I've seen my own for myself. And of course it's harder to accept the idea of someone looking out for you if you haven't experienced it. It's like if you're blind and you're in a room, I can see the chairs in the room but you can't. But they're there. To me it's almost like that. It might seem a bit strange but to me it's so natural.'

Justine's belief in a world beyond this one is a big part of her life and it's something that's part of her family life as well. Her husband, Richard, doesn't entirely share her beliefs but he knows her well enough not to dismiss them. He's had his own experiences of her insights.

'My husband doesn't come to the church or anything like that but he respects what I believe,' she says. 'One day as he was going to work, I felt really uneasy, so I asked him to call me to let me know he was okay. He was working as a window cleaner and he was normally on the ground but this particular day it turned out that he was in the cradle and it had broken as it came down the building; he could have been very badly hurt. He told me later, that he'd guessed I hadn't felt right about him going to work that day, and I really hadn't. I was very anxious. He trusts my instincts even if he doesn't understand it.'

Coincidentally, Richard's mother works as a medium, as does Justine. When they first met, Justine always had the attitude that people's spiritual beliefs were private so they never talked about them much but she says she's changed since then.

'I respected what his mum did but I didn't get involved with it,' she says. 'It's not something that I take lightly. I actually hold a service at the church, but that was only after giving birth to Trinity, not before. I always thought it was a very personal thing and I didn't want to share it but since seeing my Guardian Angel for myself, my opinion on that has shifted. If by talking about it, and bringing my experience with my angel out into the open, I might help somebody else then I think it's good to share what happened with others. Perhaps someone has felt a presence but is unsure about what that means, and if they can talk to someone about it then they won't feel as if they're the only person in the world who's experienced that sort of energy. So if sharing can help people that's good.'

Justine's attitude towards her Guardian Angel is very matter-of-fact. It doesn't seem to strike her as something particularly unusual or incredible. Her angel is just a part of her day-to-day life. She says that she regularly asks her angels for assistance, even with little things.

'I don't go out of my way to contact them but I know that they're up there so I ask them for help,' she says. 'And no matter what it is, I have a 100 per cent strike rate, they have never let me down. Never. It might take a while to get there and it's not always a straight path, but whenever I've needed help it's always been there. Sometimes it's come up in funny ways. Like I needed to get my dog's injection and I was a bit short of cash and I suddenly got a job doing paid market research for the following week! It's just silly things that happen at certain times. It can be the most mundane things as well as the really important stuff. Whatever it is, I've always had the help that I needed. And I owe that all to the help and guidance of my angels.'

Justine has also seen the nun once again since the birth of her daughter and she's confident that it wasn't for the last time.

'I wasn't very well,' she says. 'Something happened to my back and I had to use a walking stick for a bit and she came to me again. She's a constant and she's going to be with me for good.'

So far Trinity hasn't been told about the extraordinary story around her birth. Justine doesn't want her to feel pressured to believe in anything if it doesn't come naturally to her. However, she is starting to think, from some of the things that Trinity says, that her daughter might have similar gifts.

'My daughter's quite interesting because she puts colours around people's heads when she draws them, which I find funny. I wonder what that's all about.'

But Justine is extremely cautious about forcing her beliefs on to Trinity. She firmly believes that each of us has to come to faith in our own way, and takes great pains to ensure her daughter makes her own decisions about spiritual and religious matters. If angels are going to be in Trinity's life then Justine wants her to find them in her own way. However, Justine has told Trinity, in simple terms, about the other, more prosaic miracle of her conception – her in-vitro fertilisation. But that, too, she thinks had a helping hand from above.

'Richard and I have explained it to Trinity in vague terms. I told her that Mummy was helped to have her, and that we spoke to her in her little dish! She knows that she got put in Mummy's tummy,' she says. 'The funniest thing was that I was awake when I had the eggs put in. They put two embryos in and the first one went in and I didn't see anything. When the second one went in there was a flash of white light. I'm sure now that light was Trinity's spirit that I first met in my vision.'

Given how ecstatic Justine is about Trinity you might expect that she would dream about having a second child. She's very cautious about saying it but she does admit that it's something that she's thought about. In fact, after the birth of Trinity, she has had other dreams.

'I've always been given two children, a boy and a girl,' she says of those visions. 'And funnily enough, Richard and I have been tentatively speaking about the possibility of fostering. I have a feeling that there will be another child on its way one way or another but it'll make its way here when it's meant to. I'm not going to go through IVF again. If it's meant to happen it'll happen.

A final miracle for Justine is that as Trinity got older, her appearance started to change. The child who came into her arms in her vision hadn't looked very much like her daughter at all but, slowly, Justine noticed her hair getting lighter. At five years of age she looks very different to how she looked when she was born.

'The child in my dreams was blonde with blue eyes. But when my daughter was born she was quite dark with black hair. But as she's got older her hair has got lighter and her eyes have turned blue. Very much like the child I saw.'